THE ROUNDHEADS
The Good Old Cause

Aphra Behn

To the Right Noble

Henry Fitz-roy,

Duke of Grafton, Earl of Sutton, Viscount of Ipswich, Baron of Sudbury, Knight of the Most Noble Order of the Garter, and Colonel of His Majesties Regiment of Foot-guards, Etc

May it please Your Grace,

s which were Originally design'd, as a Tribute to the Reverence and just esteem we ought to pay the Great and Good ; are now so corrupted with Flattery, that they rarely either find a Reception in the World, or merit that Patronage they wou'd implore. But I without fear Approach the great Object, being above that mean and mercenary Art; nor can I draw the Lovely Picture half so charming and so manly as it is; and that Author may more properly boast of a Lucky Hitt, whose choice and Fortune is so good, than if he had pleas'd all the different ill Judging world besides in the business of the Play; for none that way, can ever hope to please all; in an Age when Faction rages, and different Parties disagree in all things— – But coming the first day to a new Play with a Loyal Title, and then even the sober and tender conscienc'd, throng as to a forbidden Conventicle, fearing the Cub of their old Bear of Reformation should be expos'd, to be the scorn of the wicked, and dreading (tho' but the faint shadow of their own deformity) their Rebellion, Murders, Massacres and Villanies, from forty upwards, should be represented for the better undeceiving and informing of the World, flock in a full Assembly with a pious design to Hiss and Rail it as much out of countenance as they would Monarchy, Religion, Laws, and Honesty; throwing the Act of Oblivion in our Teeths, as if that (whose mercy cannot make them forget their old Rebellion) cou'd hinder honest Truths from breaking out upon 'em in Edifying Plays, where the Loyal hands ever out–do their venom'd Hiss; a good and happy Omen, if Poets may be allow'd for Prophets as of old they were: and 'tis as easily seen at a new Play how the Royal Interest thrives, as at a City Election, how the Good Old Couse is carried on; as a Noble Peer lately said, Tho' the Tories have got the better of us at the Play, we carried it in the City by many Voices, God be praised!

This Play, call'd The Roundheads, which I humbly lay at your Graces feet, Pardon the Title, and Heaven defend you from the bloody Race, was carried in the House nemine contra dicente, by the Royal Party, and under your Grace's Illustrious Patronage is safe from any new Seditious affronts abroad; Your Grace alone, whom Heaven and Nature has form'd the most adorable Person in the whole Creation, with all the advantages of a glorious Birth, has a double right and power to defend all that approach you for sanctuary; your very Beauty is a Guard to all you daigne to make safe: for You were born for Conquest every way; even what Phanatick, what peevish Politician, testy with Age, Diseases, miscarried Plots, disappointed Revolutions, envious of Power, of Princes, and of Monarchy, and mad with Zeal for Change and Reformation, could yet be so far lost to sense of Pleasure, as not to turn a Rebel to Revenge the Good old Cause, and the patronage to Plebean sedition with only looking on you, 'twou'd force his meger face to blushing smiles, and make him swear he had mistook the side, curse his own Party, and if possible, be reconciled to Honesty again: such power have charms like Yours to calm the soul, and will in spight of You plead for me to the disaffected, even when they are at Wars with your Birth and Power. But this Play, for which I humbly beg your Grace's Protection, needs it in a more peculiar manner, it having drawn down Legions upon its head, for its Loyalty— what, to Name us cries one, 'tis most abominable, unheard of daring cries another— she deserves to be swing'd cries a third; as if twere all a Libel, a Scandal impossible to be prov'd, or that their Rogueries were of so old a Date their Reign were past Remembrance or History; when they take such zealous care to renew it daily to our memories: And I am satisfied, that they that will justifie the best of these Traytors, deserves the fate of the worst, and most manifestly declare to the World by it, they wou'd be at the Old Game their fore–Fathers play'd with so good success: yet if there be any honest loyal man allied to any here nam'd, I heartily beg his pardon for any offensive Truth I have spoken, and 'tis a wonderful thing that amongst so Numerous a Flock they will not allow of one mangy Sheep; not one Rogue in the whole Generation of the Association.

Ignoramus the 1st and the 2d.

But as they are I leave 'em to your Grace to Judge of 'em; to whom I humbly present this small Mirror, of the late wretched Times: wherein your Grace may see something of the Miseries three the Most Glorious Kingdoms of the Universe were reduc'd to; where your Royal Ancestors victoriously Reign'd for so many hundred years: How they were Governed, Parcell'd out, and deplorably inslav'd, and to what Low, Prostituted Lewdness they fell at last: where the Nobility and Gentry were the most contemn'd and despis'd part of them, and such Meane (and till then obscure) Villains Rul'd, and Tyrannized, that no Age, nor Time, or scarce a Parish Book makes mentions or cou'd show there was any such Name or Family. Yet these were those that impudently Tug'd for Empire, and Prophan'd that illustrious Throne and Court, so due then, and possest now (through the infinite Mercies of God to this bleeding Nation) by the best of Monarchs; a Monarch, who had the divine goodness to Pardon even his worst of Enemies what was past; Nay, out of his Vast and God–like Clemency, did more than Heaven it self can do, put it out of his Power by an Act of Oblivion, to punish the unparalell'd Injuries done His Sacred Person, and the rest of the Royal Family: How great his Patience has been since, I leave to all the World to judge: but Heaven be prais'd, he has not yet forgot the Sufferings and Murders of the Glorious Martyr of ever Blessed memory, Your Graces Sacred Grandfather, and by what Arts and Ways that Devilish Plot was layed! and will like a skilful Pilate, by the wreck of one Rich Vessel, learn how to shun the danger of this present Threatning and save the rest from sinking; The Clouds already begin to disappear, and the face of things to change, thanks to Heaven, his Majesties infinite Wisdom, and the Over–Zeal of the (falsly called) True Protestant Party; Now we may pray for the King and his Royal Brother, defend his Cause, and assert his Right, without the fear of a taste of the Old Sequestration call'd a Fine; Guard the Illustrious Pair, good Heaven, from Hellish Plots, and all the Devilish Machinations of Factious Cruelties: and you, great Sir, (whose Merits have so Justly deserv'd that glorious Command so lately trusted to your Care, which Heaven increase, and make your glad Regiment Armies for our safety. May you become the great Example of Loyalty and Obedience, and stand a firm and unmoveable Pillar to Monarchy, a Noble Bullwark to Majesty; defend the Sacred Cause, imploy all that Youth, Courage, and Noble Conduct which God and Nature purposely has endued you with, to serve the Royal Interest: You, Sir, who are obliged by a double Duty to Love, Honour, and Obey his Majesty, both as a Father and a King! O undissolvable Knot! O Sacred Union! what Duty, what Love, what Adoration can express or repay the Debt we owe the first, or the Allegiance due to the last, but where both meet in one, to make the Tye Eternal; Oh what Counsel, what Love of Power, what fancied Dreams of Empire, what fickle Popularity can inspire the heart of Man, or any Noble mind, with Sacrilegious thoughts against it, can harbour or conceive a stubborn disobedience: Oh what Son can desert the Cause of an Indulgent Parent, what Subject, of such a Prince, without renouncing the Glory of his Birth, his Loyalty, and good Nature.

Ah Royal lovely Youth! beware of false Ambition; wisely believe your Elevated Glory, (at least) more happy then a Kings, you share their Joys, their pleasures and magnificence, without the toils and business of a Monarch, their carefull days and restless thoughtfull nights; know, you art blest with all that Heaven can give, or you can wish; your Mind and Person such, so excellent, that Love knows no fault it would wish to mend, nor Envy to increase! blest with a Princess of such undisputable charming Beauty, as if Heaven, designing to take a peculiar care in all that concerns your Happiness, had form'd her on purpose, to compleat it.

Hail happy glorious Pair! the perfect joy and pleasure of all that look on ye, for whom all Tongues and Hearts have Prayers and Blessings; May you out–live Sedition, and see your Princely Race as Numerous as Beautifull, and those all great and Loyal Supporters of a long Race of Monarchs of this Sacred Line, This shall be the perpetual wish, this the Eternal Prayer of

ARGUMENT

The historical state of affairs 1659–60 was briefly as follows:— the Protectorate of Richard Cromwell expired 22 April, 1659. Hereupon Fleetwood and some other officers recalled the Long Parliament (Rump), which was constituted the ruling power of England, a select council of state having the executive. Lambert, however, with other dissentients was expelled from Parliament, 12 October, 1659. He and his troops marched to Newcastle; but the soldiers deserted him for General Fairfax, who had declared for a free Parliament, and were garrisoned at York. Here Monk, entering England 2 January, 1660, joined them with his forces. Lambert, deprived of his followers, was obliged to return to London. His prompt arrest by order of Parliament followed, and he, Sir Harry Vane and other members of the Committee of Safety were placed in strict confinement. On 5 March Lambert was imprisoned in the Tower, whence he escaped on 10 April, only to be recaptured a fortnight later. There are vivid pictures in Aubrey, Pepys, and other writers, of the wild enthusiasm at the fall of the Rump Parliament, with bonfires blazing, all the church bells ringing, and the populace of London carousing and pledging King Charles on their knees in the street. 'They made little gibbets and roasted rumps of mutton. Nay, I saw some very good rumps of beef,' writes Aubrey, and Pepys is even more vivid in his tale than the good antiquary.

King Charles landed at Dover, 26 May, amid universal rejoicings.

Mrs. Behn has (quite legitimately) made considerable departures from strict historical fact and the sequence of events for her dramatic purposes.

Lambert and Fleetwood are scheming for the supreme power, and both intrigue with Lord Wariston, the chairman of the Committee of Safety, for his good word and influence. Lambert meantime fools Fleetwood by flattery and a feigned indifference. Lady Lambert, who is eagerly expecting her husband to be proclaimed King, and is assuming the state and title of royalty to the anger of Cromwell's widow, falls in love with a cavalier, Loveless. Her friend, Lady Desbro', a thorough loyalist at heart, though wedded to an old parliamentarian, has long been enamoured of Freeman, the cavalier's companion. Lambert surprises Loveless and Freeman with his wife and Lady Desbro', but Lady Lambert pretending they have come to petition her, abruptly dismisses them both and so assuages all suspicion. At a meeting of the Committee the two gallants are sent to prison for a loyal outburst on the part of Loveless. Ananias Goggle, a lay elder, who having offered liberties to Lady Desbro' is in her power, is by her obliged to obtain her lover's release, and she at once holds an interview with him. They are interrupted by Desbro' himself, but Freeman is concealed and makes an undiscovered exit behind the shelter of Goggle's flowing cloak.

Loveless is brought to Lady Lambert at night. She endeavours to dazzle him by showing the regalia richly set out and adorned with lights. He puts by, however, crown and sceptre and rebukes her overweening ambition. Suddenly the Committee, who have been drinking deep, burst in upon them dancing a riotous dance. Loveless is hurriedly concealed under the coverlet of a couch, and Lady Lambert sits thereon seemingly at her devotions. Her husband takes his place by her side, but rolls off as the gallant slips to the ground. The lights fall down and are extinguished, the men fly howling and bawling 'A Plot! A Plot!' in drunken terror. Lambert is cajoled and hectored into believing himself mistaken owing to his potations. The ladies hold a council to correct and enquire into women's wrongs, but on a sudden, news is brought that Lambert's followers have turned against him and that he is imprisoned in the Tower. The city rises against the Parliament and the Rump is dissolved. Loveless and Freeman rescue Lady Lambert and Lady Desbro', whose old husband has fallen down dead with fright. The parliamentarians endeavour to escape, but Wariston, Goggle, and Hewson— a leading member of the Committee— are detected and maltreated by the mob. As they are haled away to prison the people give themselves up to general merry-making and joy.

SOURCE

The purely political part of The Roundheads; or, The Good Old Cause was founded by Mrs. Behn on John Tatham's The Rump; or, The Mirror of the Late Times (4to, 1660, 4to, 1661, and again 1879 in his collected works,) which was produced on the eve of the Restoration, in February, 1660, at the Private House, i.e. small theatre, in Dorset Court. The company which played here had been brought together by William Beeston, but singularly little is known of its brief career and only one name has been recorded, that of George Jolly, the leading actor. Tatham was the author of the Lord Mayor's pageants 1657–64. His plays, four in number, together with a rare entertainment, London's Glory (1660), have been well edited by Maidment and Logan.

The Rump met with great success. It is certainly a brisk and lively piece, and coming at the juncture it did must have been extraordinarily effective. As a topical key–play reflecting the moment it is indeed admirable, and the crescendo of overwhelming satire, all the keener for the poet's deep earnestness, culminating in the living actors, yesterday's lords and law–givers, running to and fro the London streets, one bawling 'Ink or pens, ink or pens!', another 'Boots or shoes, boots or shoes to mend!', a third 'Fine Seville oranges, fine lemons!', whilst Mrs. Cromwell exchanges Billingsgate with a crowd of jeering boys, must have caused the house absolutely to rock with merriment.

With all its point and cleverness The Rump, however, from a technical point of view, is ill–digested and rough. The scenes were evidently thrown off hastily, and sadly lack refining and revision. Mrs. Behn has made the happiest use of rather unpromising material. The intrigues between Loveless and Lady Lambert, who in Tatham is very woodeny and awkward, between Freeman and Lady Desbro', which give The Roundheads unity and dramatic point, are entirely her own invention. In the original Rump neither cavaliers nor Lady Desbro' appear. Ananias Goggle also, the canting lay elder of Clements, with his subtle casuistry that jibs at 'the person not the office,' a dexterous character sketch, alive and acute, we owe to Mrs. Behn.

Amongst the many plays, far too numerous even to catalogue, that scarify the puritans and their zealot tribe, The Cheats (1662), by Wilson, and Sir Robert Howard's The Committee (1662), which long kept the stage, and, in a modified form, The Honest Thieves, was seen as late as the second half of the nineteenth century, are pre–eminently the best. Both possess considerable merit and are worthy of the highest comic traditions of the theatre.

As might have been expected, the dissolution of the Rump Parliament let loose a flood of political literature, squibs, satires and lampoons. Such works as The famous Tragedie of the Life and Death of Mrs. Rump …as it was presented on a burning stage at Westminster, the 29th of May, 1660 (4to, 1660), are of course valueless save from a purely historical interest. A large number of songs and ballads were brought together and published in two parts, 1662, reprint 1874. This collection (The Rump), sometimes witty, sometimes angry, sometimes obscene, is weighty evidence of the loathing inspired by the republicans and their misrule, but it is of so personal and topical a nature that the allusions would hardly be understood by any one who had not made a very close and extended study of those critical months.

THEATRICAL HISTORY

The Roundheads; or, The Good Old Cause was produced at the Duke's Theatre in 1682. They were unsettled and hazardous times. The country was convulsed by the judicial murders and horrors which followed in the train of the pseudo–Popish Plot engineered by the abominable Gates and his accomplices. King and Parliament were at hopeless variance. The air was charged with strife, internecine hatreds and unrest. In such an atmosphere and in such circumstances politics could not but make themselves keenly felt upon the stage. The actors were indeed 'abstracts and brief chronicles of the time', and the theatre became a very Armageddon for the poets. As A Lenten Prologue refus'd by the Players (1682) puts it:— 'Plots and Parties give new matter birth And State distractions serve you here for mirth! . . . . . The Stage, like old Rump Pulpits, is become The scene of News, a furious Party's drum.'

Produced on 4 December, 1682, Dryden and Lee's excellent Tragedy, The Duke of Guise, which the Whigs vainly tried to suppress, created a furore. Crowne's City Politics (1683) is a crushing satire, caricaturing Oates, Stephen College, old Sergeant Maynard and their faction with rare skill. Southerne's Loyal Brother (1682), eulogizes the Duke of York; the scope of D'Urfey's Sir Barnaby Whigg (1681), can be told by its title, indeed the prologue says of the author:— 'That he shall know both parties now he glories, By hisses th' Whigs, and by their claps the Tories.' His Royalist (1682) follows in the same track.

Even those plays which were entirely non–political are inevitably prefaced with a mordant prologue or wound up by an epilogue that has party venom and mustard in its tail.

It would be surprising if so popular a writer as Mrs. Behn had not put a political play on the stage at such a juncture, and we find her well to the fore with The Roundheads, which she followed up in the same year with The City Heiress, another openly topical comedy.

The cast of The Roundheads is not given in any printed copy, and we have no exact means of apportioning the characters, which must have entailed the whole comic strength of the house. It is known that Betterton largely refrained from appearing in political comedies, and no doubt Smith took the part of Loveless, whilst Freeman would have fallen to Joseph Williams. Nokes was certainly Lambert; and Leigh, Wariston. Mrs. Leigh probably played Lady Cromwell or Gilliflower; Mrs. Barry, Lady Lambert; and Mrs. Currer, Lady Desbro'. The piece seems to have been very successful, and to have kept the stage at intervals for some twenty years.

PROLOGUE,

Spoken by the Ghost of Hewson ascending from Hell dress'd as a Cobler.

_I am the Ghost of him who was a true Son

Of the late Good Old Cause, ycleped Hewson,

Rous'd by strange Scandal from th' eternal Flame

With noise of Plots, of wondrous Birth and Name,

Whilst the sly Jesuit robs us of our Fame.

Can all their Conclave, tho with Hell th' agree,

Act Mischief equal to Presbytery?

Look back on our Success in Forty One,

Were ever braver Villanies carried on,

Or new ones now more hopefully begun?

And shall our Unsuccess our Merit lose,

And make us quit the Glory of our Cause?

No, hire new Villains, Rogues without Remorse,

And let no Law nor Conscience stop your Course;

Let Politicians order the Confusion,

And let the Saints pay pious Contribution.

Pay those that rail, and those that can delude

With scribling Nonsense the loose Multitude.

Pay well your Witnesses, they may not run

To the right Side, and tell who set 'em on.

Pay 'em so well, that they may ne'er recant,

And so turn honest merely out of want.

Pay Juries, that no formal Laws may harm us,

Let Treason be secur'd by Ignoramus.

Pay Bully Whig, who loyal Writers bang,

And honest Tories in Effigie hang:

Pay those that burn the Pope to please the Fools,

And daily pay Right Honourable Tools;

Pay all the Pulpit Knaves that Treason brew,

And let the zealous Sisters pay 'em too;

Justices, bound by Oath and Obligation,

Pay them the utmost Price of their Damnation,

Not to disturb our useful Congregation.

Nor let the Learned Rabble be forgot,

Those pious Hands that crown our hopeful Plot.

No, modern Statesmen cry, 'tis Lunacy

To barter Treason with such Rogues as we.

But subtiler Oliver did not disdain

His mightier Politicks with ours to join.

I for all Uses in a State was able,

Cou'd Mutiny, cou'd fight, hold forth, and cobble.

Your lazy Statesman may sometimes direct,

But your small busy Knaves the Treason act._

DRAMATIS PERSONÆ

Men

Lord Fleetwood, } Competitors for the Crown, Lord Lambert, } but Lambert is General of the Army. Lord Wariston, Chairman of the Committee of Safety. Hewson, } Desbro, } Commanders, Duckingfield, } and Committee–men. Corbet, } Lord Whitlock. Ananias Goggle, Lay Elder of Clement's Parish. A Rabble of the Sanctify'd Mobile. Corporal Right, an Oliverian Commander, but honest, and a Cavalier in his Heart. Loveless, a Royalist, a Man of Honour, in love with Lady Lambert. Freeman, his Friend, of the same Character, in love with Lady Desbro. Captain of the Prentices. Two Pages to Lady Lambert. Tom, Page to Lady Desbro. Page to Lady Fleetwood. A Felt–maker. A Joyner. Doorkeeper. Two Clerks. Three Soldiers.

WOMEN.

Lady Lambert, in love with Loveless.

Lady Desbro, in love with Freeman.

Lady Fleetwood.

Lady Cromwell.

Gilliflower, Lady Lambert's Old Woman.

Several Ladies, for Redress of Grievances.

Women Servants to Lady Lambert.

Petitioners, Servants, Guards, Footmen, Fidlers, and a Band of Loyal City Apprentices.

ACT I

SCENE I. The Street.

Enter three Soldiers, and Corporal Right.

Cor. Ah, Rogue, the World runs finely round, the business is done.

1 Sold. Done! the Town's our own, my fine Rascal.

2 Sold. We'll have Harlots by the Belly, Sirrah.

1 Sold. Those are Commodities I confess I wou'd fain be trucking for— but no words of that, Boy.

Cor. Stand, who goes there?

[To them a Joyner and a Felt–maker.

1 Sold. Who are you for?— hah!

Joy. Are for, Friend? we are for Gad and the Lord Fleetwood.

1 Sold. Fleetwood! knock 'em down, Fleetwood, that sniveling Thief?

Felt. Why, Friends, who are ye for?

Cor. For! who shou'd we be for, but Lambert, Noble Lambert? Is this a time o'th' day to declare for Fleetwood, with a Pox? indeed, i'th' Morning 'twas a Question had like to have been decided with push a Pike.

2 Sold. Dry blows wou'd ne'er ha' don't, some must have sweat Blood for't; but— 'tis now decided.

Joy. Decided!

2 Sold. Yes, decided, Sir, without your Rule for't.

Joy. Decided! by whom, Sir? by us the Free–born Subjects of England, by the Honourable Committee of Safety, or the Right Reverend City? without which, Sir, I humbly conceive, your Declaration for Lambert is illegal, and against the Property of the People.

2 Sold. Plain Lambert; here's a saucy Dog of a Joyner; Sirrah, get ye home, and mind your Trade, and save the Hangman a labour.

Joy. Look ye, Friend, I fear no Hang–man in Christendom; for Conscience and Publick Good, for Liberty and Property, I dare as far as any Man.

2 Sold. Liberty and Property, with a Pox, in the Mouth of a Joyner: you are a pretty Fellow to settle the Nation— what says my Neighbour Felt–maker?

Felt. Why, verily, I have a high respect for my honourable Lord Fleetwood, he is my intimate Friend; and till I find his Party the weaker, I hope my Zeal will be strengthned for him.

2 Sold. Zeal for Fleetwood! Zeal for a Halter, and that's your due: Why, what has he ever done for you? Can he lead you out to Battle? Can he silence the very Cannon with his Eloquence alone?— Can he talk— or fight— or—

Felt. But verily he can pay those that can, and that's as good— and he can pray—

2 Sold. Let him pray, and we'll fight, and see whose business is done first; we are for the General who carries Charms in every Syllable; can act both the Soldier and the Courtier, at once expose his Breast to Dangers for our sakes— and tell the rest of the pretended Slaves a fair Tale, but hang 'em sooner than trust 'em.

1 Sold. Ay, ay, a Lambert, a Lambert, he has Courage, Fleetwood's an Ass to him.

Felt. Hum— here's Reason, Neighbour. [To the Joyner.

Joy. That's all one, we do not act by Reason.

Cor. Fleetwood's a Coward.

2 Sold. A Blockhead.

1 Sold. A sniveling Fool; a General in the Hangings, no better.

Joy. What think you then of Vane?

2 Sold. As of a Fool, that has dreamt of a new Religion, and is only fit to reign in the Fifth Monarchy he preaches so much up? but no King in this Age.

Felt. What of Haslerig?

2 Sold. A Hangman for Haslerig. I cry, No, no, One and all, a Lambert, a Lambert; he is our General, our Protector, our Keiser, our— even what he pleases himself.

1 Sold. Well, if he pleases himself, he pleases me.

2 Sold. He's our Rising Sun, and we'll adore him, for the Speaker's Glory's set.

Cor. At nought, Boys; how the Rogue look'd when his Coach was stop'd!

Joy. Under favour, what said the Speaker?

2 Sold. What said he? prithee, what cou'd he say that we wou'd admit for Reason? Reason and our Bus'ness are two things: Our Will was Reason and Law too, and the Word of Command lodg'd in our Hilts: Cobbet and Duckenfield shew'd 'em Cockpit—Law.

Cor. He understood not Soldier's Dialect; the Language of the Sword puzzled his Understanding; the Keenness of which was too sharp for his Wit, and over—rul'd his Robes— therefore he very mannerly kiss'd his Hand, and wheel'd about—

2 Sold. To the place from whence he came.

Cor. And e'er long to the place of Execution.

1 Sold. No, damn him, he'll have his Clergy.

Joy. Why, is he such an Infidel to love the Clergy?

Cor. For his Ends; but come let's go drink the General's Health, Lambert; not Fleetwood, that Son of a Custard, always quaking.

2 Sold. Ay, ay, Lambert I say— besides, he's a Gentleman.

Felt. Come, come, Brother Soldier, let me tell you, I fear you have a Stewart in your Belly.

Cor. I am sure you have a Rogue in your Heart, Sirrah, which a Man may perceive thro that sanctified Dog's Face of yours; and so get ye gone, ye Rascals, and delude the Rabble with your canting Politicks. [Every one beats 'em.

Felt. Nay, an you be in Wrath, I'll leave you.

Joy. No matter, Sir, I'll make you know I'm a Freeborn Subject, there's Law for the Righteous, Sir, there's Law. [Go out.

Cor. There's Halters, ye Rogues—

2 Sold. Come, Lads, let's to the Tavern, and drink Success to Change; I doubt not but to see 'em chop about, till it come to our great Hero again— Come to the Tavern.

[Going out, are met by Loveless and Freeman, who enter, and stay the Corporal.

Cor. I'll follow ye, Comrade, presently.

[Ex. the rest of the Soldiers.

—Save ye, noble Colonel.

Free. How is't, Corporal?

Cor. A brave World, Sir, full of Religion, Knavery, and Change: we shall shortly see better Days.

Free. I doubt it, Corporal.

Cor. I'll warrant you, Sir,— but have you had never a Billet, no Present, nor Love— remembrance to day, from my good Lady Desbro?

Free. None, and wonder at it. Hast thou not seen her Page to day?

Cor. Faith, Sir, I was imploy'd in Affairs of State, by our Protector that shall be, and could not call.

Free. Protector that shall be! who's that, Lambert, or Fleetwood, or both?

Cor. I care not which, so it be a Change; but I mean the General:— but, Sir, my Lady Desbro is now at Morning–Lecture here hard by, with the Lady Lambert.

Lov. Seeking the Lord for some great Mischief or other.

Free. We have been there, but could get no opportunity of speaking to her— Loveless, know this Fellow— he's honest and true to the Hero, tho a Red–Coat. I trust him with my Love, and have done with my Life.

Lov. Love! Thou canst never make me believe thou art earnestly in love with any of that damn'd Reformation.

Free. Thou art a Fool; where I find Youth and Beauty, I adore, let the Saint be true or false.

Lov. 'Tis a Scandal to one of us to converse with 'em; they are all sanctify'd Jilts; and there can neither be Credit nor Pleasure in keeping 'em company; and 'twere enough to get the Scandal of an Adherer to their devilish Politicks, to be seen with 'em.

Free. What, their Wives?

Lov. Yes, their Wives. What seest thou in 'em but Hypocrisy? Make love to 'em, they answer in Scripture.

Free. Ay, and lie with you in Scripture too. Of all Whores, give me your zealous Whore; I never heard a Woman talk much of Heaven, but she was much for the Creature too. What do'st think I had thee to the Meeting for?

Lov. To hear a Rascal hold forth for Bodkins and Thimbles, Contribution, my beloved! to carry on the good Cause, that is, Roguery, Rebellion, and Treason, profaning the sacred Majesty of Heaven, and our glorious Sovereign.

Free. But— were there not pretty Women there?

Lov. Damn 'em for sighing, groaning Hypocrites.

Free. But there was one, whom that handsome Face and Shape of yours, gave more occasion for sighing, than any Mortification caus'd by the Cant of the Lay–Elder in the half Hogs–Head: Did'st thou not mind her?

Lov. Not I, damn it, I was all Rage; and hadst not thou restrain'd me, I had certainly pull'd that Rogue of a Holder forth by the Ears from his sanctify'd Tub. 'Sdeath, he hum'd and haw'd all my Patience away, nosed and snivel'd me to Madness. Heaven! That thou shouldst suffer such Vermin to infect the Earth, such Wolves amongst thy Flocks, such Thieves and Robbers of all Laws of God and Man, in thy Holy Temples. I rave to think to what thou'rt fall'n, poor England!

Free. But the she Saint—

Lov. No more; were she as fair as Fancy could imagine, to see her there wou'd make me loath the Form; she that can listen to the dull Nonsense, the bantering of such a Rogue, such an illiterate Rascal, must be a Fool, past sense of loving, Freeman.

Free. Thou art mistaken.— But, didst thou mind her next the Pulpit?

Lov. A Plague upon the whole Congregation: I minded nothing but how to fight the Lord's Battle with that damn'd sham Parson, whom I had a mind to beat.

Free. My Lady Desbro is not of that Persuasion, but an errant Heroick in her Heart, and feigns it only to have the better occasion to serve the Royal Party. I knew her, and lov'd her before she married.

Lov. She may chance then to be sav'd.

Free. Come, I'll have thee bear up briskly to some one of 'em, it may redeem thy Sequestration; which, now thou see'st no hopes of compounding, puts thee out of Patience.

Lov. Let 'em take it, and the Devil do 'em Good with it; I scorn it should be said I have a Foot of Land in this ungrateful and accursed Island; I'd rather beg where Laws are obey'd, and Justice perform'd, than be powerful where Rogues and base–born Rascals rule the roast.

Free. But suppose now, dear Loveless, that one of the Wives of these Pageant Lords should fall in love with thee, and get thy Estate again, or pay the double for't?

Lov. I wou'd refuse it.

Free. And this for a little dissembl'd Love, a little Drudgery—

Lov. Not a Night, by Heaven— not an Hour— no, not a single Kiss. I'd rather make love to an Incubus.

Free. But suppose 'twere the new Protectress her self, the fine Lady Lambert?

Lov. The greatest Devil of all; damn her, do'st think I'll cuckold the Ghost of old Oliver?

Free. The better; There's some Revenge in't; do'st know her?

Lov. Never saw her, nor care to do.

Cor. Colonel, do you command me any thing?

Free. Yes, I'll send thee with a Note— Let's step into a Shop and write it; Loveless, stay a moment, and I'll be with thee. [Ex. Free. and Corporal.

Enter L. Lambert, L. Desbro, Gilliflower, Pages with great

Bibles, and Footmen. Loveless walks sullenly, not seeing 'em.

[L. Lambert's Train carried.

L. Lam. O, I'm impatient to know his Name; ah, Desbro, he betray'd all my Devotion; and when I would have pray'd, Heav'n knows it was to him, and for him only.

L. Des. What manner of Man was it?

L. Lam. I want Words to describe him; not tall, nor short; well made, and such a Face— Love, Wit and Beauty revel'd in his Eyes; From whence he shot a thousand winged Darts That pierc'd quite through my Soul.

L. Des. Seem'd he a Gentleman?

L. Lam. A God! altho his outside were but mean; But he shone thro like Lightning from a Cloud, And shot more piercing Rays.

19

L. Des. Staid he long?

L. Lam. No, methought he grew displeas'd with our Devotion, And seem'd to contradict the Parson with his angry Eyes. A Friend he had too with him, young and handsom, Who seeing some Disorder in his Actions, got him away. —I had almost forgot all Decency, And started up to call him; but my Quality, And wanting something to excuse that Fondness, Made me decline with very much ado.

Gill. Heavens, Madam, I'll warrant they were Heroicks.

L. Lam. Heroicks!

Gill. Cavaliers, Madam, of the Royal Party.

L. Des. They were so, I knew one of 'em.

L. Lam. Ah, Desbro, do'st thou? Ah, Heav'ns, that they should prove Heroicks!

L. Des. You might have known that by the Conquest; I never heard any one o't' other Party ever gain'd a Heart; and indeed, Madam, 'tis a just Revenge, our Husbands make Slaves of them, and they kill all their Wives. [Lov. sees 'em, and starts.

Lov. Hah, what have we here?— Women— faith, and handsome too— I never saw a Form more excellent; who e'er they are, they seem of Quality.— By Heav'n, I cannot take my Eyes from her. [Pointing to L. Lamb.

L. Lam. Ha, he's yonder, my Heart begins to fail, My trembling Limbs refusing to support me— His Eyes seem fix'd on mine too; ah, I faint— [Leans on Des.

Gill. My Lady's Coach, William— quickly, she faints.

Lov. Madam, can an unfortunate Stranger's aid add any thing to the recovery of so much Beauty? [Bowing, and holding her.

L. Lam. Ah, wou'd he knew how much! [Aside.

Gill. Support her, Sir, till her Ladyship's Coach comes— I beseech ye.

Lov. Not Atlas bore up Heaven with greater Pride.

L. Lam. —I beg your Pardon, Sir, for this Disorder, That has occasion'd you so great a Trouble— You seem a Gentleman— and consequently May need some Service done you; name the way, I shall be glad to let you see my Gratitude.

Lov. If there be ought in me, that merits this amazing Favour from you, I owe my Thanks to Nature that endow'd me with something in my Face that spoke my Heart.

L. Lam. Heaven! How he looks and speaks— [To Desbro, aside.

L. Des. Oh, these Heroicks, Madam, have the most charming Tongues.

L. Lam. Pray come to me— and ask for any of my Officers, and you shall have admittance—

Lov. Who shall I ask for, Madam? for I'm yet ignorant to whom I owe for this great Bounty.

L. Lam. Not know me! Thou art indeed a Stranger. I thought I'd been so elevated above the common Crowd, it had been visible to all Eyes who I was.

Lov. Pardon my Ignorance. My Soul conceives ye all that Heaven can make ye, Of Great, of Fair and Excellent; But cannot guess a Name to call you by But such as would displease ye— My Heart begins to fail, and by her Vanity I fear she's one of the new Race of Quality: —But be she Devil, I must love that Form. [Aside.

L. Lam. Hard Fate of Greatness, we so highly elevated Are more expos'd to Censure than the little ones, By being forc'd to speak our Passions first. —Is my Coach ready?

Page. It waits your Honour.

L. Lam. I give you leave to visit me— ask for the General's Lady, if my Title be not by that time alter'd.

Lov. Pistols and Daggers to my Heart— 'tis so.

L. Lam. Adieu, Sir.

[Ex. all but Lov. who stands musing.

Enter Freeman.

Free. How now, what's the matter with thee?

Lov. Prithee wake me, Freeman.

Free. Wake thee!

Lov. I dream; by Heaven I dream; Nay, yet the lovely Phantom's in my View. Oh! wake me, or I sleep to perfect Madness.

Free. What ail'st thou? what did'st dream of?

Lov. A strange fantastick Charmer, A thing just like a Woman Friend; It walkt and lookt with wondrous Majesty, Had Eyes that kill'd, and Graces deck'd her Face; But when she talk'd, mad as the Winds she grew, Chimera in the form of Angel, Woman!

Free. Who the Devil meanest thou?

Lov. By Heav'n I know not, but, as she vanish'd hence, she bad me come to the General's.

Free. Why, this is she I told thee ey'd thee so at the Conventicle; 'tis Lambert, the renown'd, the famous Lady Lambert— Mad call'st thou her? 'tis her ill acted Greatness, thou mistak'st; thou art not us'd to the Pageantry of these Women yet: they all run thus mad; 'tis Greatness in 'em, Loveless.

Lov. And is thine thus, thy Lady Desbro?

Free. She's of another Cut, she married, as most do, for Interest— but what— thou't to her?

Lov. If Lightning stop my way:— Perhaps a sober View may make me hate her. [Exeunt both.

SCENE II. A Chamber in Lambert's House.

Enter Lambert and Whitlock.

Whit. My Lord, now is your time, you may be King; Fortune is yours, you've time it self by th' Fore–lock.

Lam. If I thought so, I'd hold him fast, by Heaven.

Whit. If you let slip this Opportunity, my Lord, you are undone— Aut Cæsar, aut Nullus.

Lam. But Fleetwood—

Whit. Hang him, soft Head.

Lam. True, he's of an easy Nature; yet if thou didst but know how little Wit governs this mighty Universe, thou wou'dst not wonder Men should set up him.

Whit. That will not recommend him at this Juncto, tho he's an excellent Tool for your Lordship to make use of; and therefore use him, Sir, as Cataline did Lentulus; drill the dull Fool with Hopes of Empire on, and that all tends to his Advancement only: The Blockhead will believe the Crown his own: What other Hopes could make him ruin Richard, a Gentleman of Qualities a thousand times beyond him?

Lam. They were both too soft; an ill Commendation for a General, who should be rough as Storms of War it self.

Whit. His time was short, and yours is coming on; Old Oliver had his.

Lam. I hate the Memory of that Tyrant Oliver.

Whit. So do I, now he's dead, and serves my Ends no more. I lov'd the Father of the great Heroick, whilst he had Power to do me good: he failing, Reason directed me to the Party then prevailing, the Fag–end of the Parliament: 'tis true, I took the Oath of Allegiance, as Oliver, your Lordship, Tony, and the rest did, without which we could not have sat in that Parliament; but that Oath was not for our Advantage, and so better broke than kept.

Lam. I am of your Opinion, my Lord.

Whit. Let Honesty and Religion preach against it. But how cou'd I have serv'd the Commons by deserting the King? how have I show'd my self loyal to your Interest, by fooling Fleet–wood, in the deserting of Dick; by dissolving the honest Parliament, and bringing in the odious Rump? how cou'd I have flatter'd Ireton, by telling him Providence brought thingsabout, when 'twas mere Knavery all; and that the Hand of the Lord was in't, when I knew the Devil was in't? or indeed, how cou'd I now advise you to be King, if I had started at Oaths, or preferr'd Honesty or Divinity before Interest and the Good Old Came?

Lam. Nay,'tis most certain, he that will live in this World, must be endu'd with the three rare Qualities of Dissimulation, Equivocation, and mental Reservation.

Whit. In which Excellency, Heav'n be prais'd, we out–do the Jesuits.

Enter Lady Lambert.

L. Lam. I'm glad to see you so well employ'd, my Lord, as in Discourse with my Lord Whitlock, he's of our Party, and has Wit.

Whit. Your Honour graces me too much.

Lam. My Lord, my Lady is an absolute States–woman.

L. Lam. Yes, I think things had not arriv'd to this exalted height, nor had you been in prospect of a Crown, had not my Politicks exceeded your meaner Ambition.

Lam. I confess, I owe all my good Fortune to thee.

Enter Page.

Page. My Lord, my Lord Wariston, Lord Hewson, Colonel Cobbet, and Colonel Duckenfield desire the Honour of waiting on you.

L. Lam. This has a Face of Greatness— let 'em wait a while i'th' Antichamber.

23

Lam. My Love, I would have 'em come in.

L. Lam. You wou'd have 'em! you wou'd have a Fool's Head of your own; pray let me be Judge of what their Duty is, and what your Glory: I say I'll have 'em wait.

Page. My Lord Fleetwood too is just alighted, shall lie wait too, Madam?

L. Lam. He may approach: and d'ye hear— put on your fawning Looks, flatter him, and profess much Friendship to him, you may betray him with the more facility.

Whit. Madam, you counsel well. [Ex. Page.

Page re–enters with Lord Fleetwood.

Lam. My good Lord, your most submissive Servant.

Whit. My gracious Lord, I am your Creature— your Slave—

Fleet. I profess ingeniously, I am much engag'd to you, my good Lords; I hope things are now in the Lard's handling, and will go on well for his Glory and my Interest, and that all my good People of England will do things that become good Christians.

Whit. Doubt us not, my good Lord; the Government cannot be put into abler Hands than those of your Lordship; it has hitherto been in the hard Clutches of Jews, Infidels, and Pagans.

Fleet. Yea, verily, Abomination has been in the Hands of Iniquity.

Lam. But, my Lord, those Hands, by my good Conduct, are now cut off, and our Ambition is, your Lordship wou'd take the Government upon you.

Fleet. I profess, my Lord, by yea and nay, I am asham'd of this Goodness, in making me the Instrument of saving Grace to this Nation; 'tis the great Work of the Lard.

L. Lam. The Lard! Sir, I'll assure you the Lard has the least Hand in your good Fortune; I think you ought to ascribe it to the Cunning and Conduct of my Lord here, who so timely abandon'd the Interest of Richard.

Fleet. Ingeniously I must own, your good Lord can do much, and has done much; but 'tis our Method to ascribe all to the Powers above.

L. Lam. Then I must tell you, your Method's an ungrateful Method.

Lam. Peace, my Love.

Whit. Madam, this is the Cant we must delude the Rabble with.

L. Lam. Then let him use it there, my Lord, not amongst us, who so well understand one another.

Lam. Good Dear, be pacified— and tell me, shall the Gentlemen without have Admittance?

L. Lam. They may. [Page goes out.

Enter Hewson, Desbro, Duckenfield, Wariston, and Cobbet.

War. Guds Benizon light on yu, my gued Loords, for this Day's Work; Madam, I kiss your white Honds.

Duc. My Lord, I have not been behind–hand in this Day's turn of State.

Lam. 'Tis confess'd, Sir; what would you infer from that?

Duc. Why, I wou'd know how things go; who shall be General, who Protector?

Hews. My Friend has well translated his meaning.

L. Lam. Fy, how that filthy Cobler Lord betrays his Function.

Duc. We're in a Chaos, a Confusion, as we are.

Hews. Indeed the Commonwealth at present is out at Heels, and wants underlaying.

Cob. And the People expect something suddenly from us.

Whit. My Lords and Gentlemen, we must consider a while.

War. Bread a gued there's mickle Wisdom i'that, Sirs.

Duc. It ought to be consulted betimes, my Lord, 'tis a matter of Moment, and ought to be consulted by the whole Committee.

Lam. We design no other, my Lord, for which Reason at three a Clock we'll meet at Wallingford House.

Duc. Nay, my Lord, do but settle the Affair, let's but know who's our Head, and 'tis no matter.

Hews. Ay, my Lord, no matter who; I hope 'twill be Fleetwood, for I have the length of his Foot already.

Whit. You are the leading Men, Gentlemen, your Voices will soon settle the Nation.

Duc. Well, my Lord, we'll not fail at three a Clock.

Des. This falls out well for me; for I've Business in Smithfield, where my Horses stand; and verily, now I think on't, the Rogue the Ostler has not given 'em Oates to day: Well, my Lords, farewel; if I come not time enough to Wallingford House, keep me a Place in the Committee, and let my Voice stand for one, no matter who.

War. A gued Mon I's warrant, and takes muckle Pains for the Gued o'th' Nation, and the Liberty o'th Mobily— The Diel confound 'em aud.

Lam. Come, my Lord Wariston, you are a wise Man, what Government are you for.

War. Ene tol what ya please, my gued Loord. [Takes him aside.

Lam. What think you of a single Person here in my Lord Fleetwood?

War. Marry, Sir, and he's a brave Mon, but gen I may cooncel, tak't for yar sel my gued Loord, ant be gued for him, 'tis ene gued for ya te.

Lam. But above half the Nation are for him.

War. Bread a gued, and I's for him then.

Fleet. The Will of the Lard be done; and since 'tis his Will, I cannot withstand my Fate— ingeniously.

Whit. My Lord Wariston, a Word— What if Lambert were the Man? [Takes him aside.

War. Right Sir, Wons and ya have spoken aud; he's a brave Mon, a Mon indeed gen I's have any Judgment.

Whit. So I find this Property's for any use. [Aside.

Lam. My Lord, I perceive Heaven and Earth conspire to make you our Prince.

Fleet. Ingeniously, my Lords, the Weight of three Kingdoms is a heavy Burden for so weak Parts as mine: therefore I will, before I appear at Council, go seek the Lard in this great Affair; and if I receive a Revelation for it, I shall with all Humility espouse the Yoke, for the Good of his People and mine; and so Gad with us, the Commonwealth of England. [Exeunt Fleet. Desbro, Wariston, Due. Cob. Hews, and Whit.

L. Lam. Poor deluded Wretch, 'tis not yet come to that.

Lam. No, my dear, the Voice will go clearly for me; what with Bribes to some, Hypocrisy and Pretence of Religion to others, and promis'd Preferments to the rest, I have engag'd 'em all.

L. Lam. And will you be a King?

Lam. You think that's so fine a thing— but let me tell you, my Love, a King's a Slave to a Protector, a King's ty'd up to a thousand Rules of musty Law, which we can break at pleasure; we can rule without Parliaments, at least chuse whom we please, make 'em agree to our Proposals, or set a Guard upon 'em, and starve 'em till they do.

L. Lam. But their Votes are the strangest things— that they must pass for Laws; you were never voted King.

Lam. No, nor care to be: The sharpest Sword's my Vote, my Law, my Title. They voted Dick should reign, where is he now? They voted the great Heroicks from the Succession; but had they Arms or Men, as I have, you shou'd soon see what wou'd become of their Votes— No, my Love! 'tis this— must make me King. [His Sword. Let Fleetwood and the Rump go seek the Lard, My Empire and my Trust is in my Sword.

ACT II

SCENE I. A Chamber of State in Lambert's House.

Enter L. Lambert, Gilliflower, and Women–servants.

L. Lam. Gilliflower, has none been here to ask for any of my People, in order to his approach to me?

Gill. None, Madam.

L. Lam. Madam! How dull thou art? wo't never learn to give me a better Title than such an one as foolish Custom bestows on every common Wench?

Gill. Pardon my Ignorance, Madam.

L. Lam. Again Madam?

Gill. Really, Madam, I shou'd be glad to know by what other Title you wou'd be distinguish'd?

L. Lam. Abominable dull! Do'st thou not know on what score my Dear is gone to Wallingford House?

Gill. I cannot divine, Madam.

L. Lam. Heaven help thy Ignorance! he's gone to be made Protector, Fool, or at least a King, thou Creature; and from this Day I date my self her Highness.

Gill. That will be very fine indeed, an't please your Highness.

L. Lam. I think 'twill sute better with my Person and Beauty than with the other Woman— what d'ye call her? Mrs. Cromwell— my Shape— and Gate— my Humour, and my Youth have something more of Grandeur, have they not?

Gill. Infinitely, an't please your Highness.

Enter Page.

Page. Madam, a Man without has the boldness to ask for your Honour.

L. Lam. Honour, Fool!

Gill. Her Highness, Blockhead.

Page. Saucily prest in, and struck the Porter for denying him entrance to your— Highness.

L. Lam. What kind of Fellow was't?

Page. A rude, rough, hectoring Swash, an't please your Highness; nay, and two or three times, Gad forgive me, he swore too.

L. Lam. It must be he. [Aside.

Page. His Habit was something bad and Cavalierish— I believe 'twas some poor petitioning, begging Tory, who having been sequester'd, wou'd press your Highness for some Favour.

L. Lam. Yes, it must be he— ah, foolish Creature! and can he hope Relief, and be a villanous Cavalier? out upon 'em, poor Wretches— you may admit him tho', for I long to hear how one of those things talk.

Gill. Oh, most strangely, Madam— an please your Highness, I shou'd say.

Enter Loveless.

L. Lam. 'Tis he, I'll swear, Gilliflower, these Heroicks are punctual men— how now, your Bus'ness with us, Fellow?

Lov. My Bus'ness, Madam?—

L. Lam. Hast thou ever a Petition to us?

Lov. A Petition, Madam?— Sure this put— on Greatness is to amuse her Servants, or has she forgot that she invited me? or indeed forgot me?— [Aside.

L. Lam. What art thou?

Page. Shall we search his Breeches, an't please your Highness, for Pistol, or other Instruments?

L. Lam. No, Boy, we fear him not, they say the Powers above protect the Persons of Princes. [Walks away.

Lov. Sure she's mad, yet she walks loose about, And she has Charms even in her raving Fit.

L. Lam. Answer me. What art thou?— How shall I get my Servants hence with Honour? [Aside.

Lov. A Gentleman— That could have boasted Birth and Fortune too, Till these accursed Times, which Heaven confound, Razing out all Nobility, all Virtue, Has render'd me the rubbish of the World; Whilst new rais'd Rascals, Canters, Robbers, Rebels, Do lord it o'er the Free–born, Brave and Noble.

L. Lam. You're very confident, know you to whom you speak? but I suppose you have lost your Estate, or some such trivial thing, which makes you angry.

Lov. Yes, a trivial Estate of some five and twenty hundred Pound a Year: but I hope to see that Rogue of a Lord reduc'd to his Cobler's–Stall again, or more deserv'dly hang'd, that has it.

L. Lam. I thought 'twas some such Grievance— but you must keep a good Tongue in your Head, lest you be hang'd for Scandalum Magnatum— there's Law for ye, Sir.

Lov. No matter, then I shall be free from a damn'd Commonwealth, as you are pleas'd to call it, when indeed 'tis but a mungrel, mangy, Mock–Monarchy.

L. Lam. Is it your business, Sir, to rail?

Lov. You rais'd the Devil, Madam.

Page. Madam, shall I call your Highness's Guards, and secure the Traitor?

L. Lam. No, that you may see how little I regard or fear him; leave us all— [Ex. all but Gill. We'll trust our Person in his Hands alone— —Now, Sir— Your Bus'ness? [Smilingly approaches him.

Lav. Madam, I waited here by your Commands.

L. Lam. How shall I tell him that I love him, Gilliflower?

Gill. Easily, Madam, tell him so in plain English. Madam,'tis great; Women of your exalted height ever speak first; you have no Equals dare pretend to speak of Love to you.

L. Lam. Thou art i'th' right— Do'st know my Quality, and thy own Poverty? And hast thou nothing to ask that I may grant?

Lav. Sure she loves me! and I, frail Flesh and Blood, Cannot resist her Charms; but she's of the damn'd Party. [Aside.

L. Lam. Are all your Party, Sir, so proud?

Lov. But what have I to do with Religion! Is Beauty the worse, or a kind Wench to be refus'd for Conventickling? She lives high on the Spoils of a glorious Kingdom, and why may not I live upon the Sins of the Spoiler? [Aside.

L. Lam. Sir— you are poor!

Lov. So is my Prince; a Plague on the occasion.

L. Lam. I think you are— no Fool too.

Lov. I wou'd I were, then I had been a Knave, had thriv'd, and possibly by this time had been tugging for rifled Crowns and Kingdoms.

L. Lam. This Satir ill befits my present Bus'ness with you— you— want some Necessaries— as Clothes, and Linen too; and 'tis great pity so proper a Man shou'd want Necessaries. Gilliflower— take my Cabinet Key, and fetch the Purse of Broad–pieces that lies in the lower Drawer; 'tis a small Present, Sir, but 'tis an Earnest of my farther Service. [Gill. goes out and returns with a Purse.

Lov. I'm angry, that I find one Grain of Generosity in this whole Race of Hypocrites. [Aside.

L. Lam. Here, Sir,'tis only for your present use; for Clothes— three hundred Pieces; let me see you sweet—

Lov. Stark mad, by this good Day.

L. Lam. Ah, Gilliflower! How prettily those Cavalier things charm; I wonder how the Powers above came to give them all the Wit, Softness, and Gallantry— whilst all the great ones of our Age have the most slovenly, ungrateful, dull Behaviour; no Air, no Wit, no Love, nor any thing to please a Lady with.

Gill. Truly, Madam, there's a great Difference in the Men; yet Heaven at first did its part, but the Devil has since so over–done his, that what with the Vizor of Sanctity, which is the gadly Sneer, the drawing of the Face to a prodigious length, the formal Language, with a certain Twang through the Nose, and the pious Gogle, they are fitter to scare Children than beget love in Ladies.

Lav. You hit the Character of your new Saint.

L. Lam. And then their Dress, Gilliflower.

Gil. Oh! 'Tis an Abomination to look like a Gentleman; long Hair is wicked and cavalierish, a Periwig is flat Popery, the Disguise of the Whore of Babylon; handsom Clothes, or lac'd Linen, the very Tempter himself, that debauches all their Wives and Daughters; therefore the diminutive Band, with the Hair of the Reformation Cut, beneath which a pair of large sanctify'd Souses appear, to declare to the World they had hitherto escap'd the Pillory, tho deserv'd it as well as Pryn.

L. Lam. Have a care what you say, Gilliflower.

Gil. Why, Madam, we have no Informers here.

Enter Page.

Page. Madam, here's Old Noll's Wife desires Admittance to your Hon— your Highness.

L. Lam. Bid the poor Creature wait without, I'll do her what Good I can for her Husband's sake, who first infus'd Politicks into me, by which I may boast I have climb'd to Empire.

Lov. So, her Madness runs in that Vein I see. [Aside.

Gil. Alack, Madam, I think she's coming.

Crom. [without] Does she keep State in the Devil's Name, and must I wait?

L. Lam. Heavens! I shall be scandalized by the Godly. Dear Gilliflower, conceal my Cavalier; I would not have a Cavalier seen with me for all the World— Step into my Cabinet. [Ex. Gil. and Lov.

Enter L. Cromwel, held back by a Man— to them Gilliflower.

Crom. Unhand me, Villain— 'twas not long since a Rudeness, Sir, like this had forfeited thy Head.

L. Lam. What wou'd the Woman?

Crom. The Knave, the perjur'd Villain thy Husband, by th' Throat: thou proud, imperious Baggage, to make me wait; whose Train thou hast been proud to bear— how durst thou, after an Affront like this, trust thy false Face within my Fingers reach? that Face, that first bewitch'd the best of Husbands from me, and tempted him to sin.

Gil. I beseech your Highness retire, the Woman's mad.

Crom. Highness in the Devil's Name, sure 'tis not come to that; no, I may live to see thy Cuckold hang'd first, his Politicks are yet too shallow, Mistress. Heavens! Did my Husband make him Lord for this? raise him to Honour, Trusts, Commands, and Counsels, To ruin all our Royal Family, Betray young Richard, who had reign'd in Peace But for his Perjuries and Knaveries; And now he sooths my Son–in–law, soft Fleetwood, With empty hopes of Pow'r, and all the while To make himself a King: No, Minion, no; I yet may live to see Thy Husband's Head o'th' top of Westminster, Before I see it circled in a Crown.

L. Lam. I pity the poor Creature.

Crom. Ungrateful Traytor as he is, Not to look back upon his Benefactors; But he, in lieu of making just Returns, Reviles our Family, profanes our Name, And will in time render it far more odious Than ever Needham made the great Heroicks.

L. Lam. Alas, it weeps, poor Woman!

32

Crom. Thou ly'st, false Strumpet, I scorn to shed a Tear, For ought that thou canst do or say to me; I've too much of my Husband's Spirit in me. Oh, my dear Richard, hadst thou had a Grain on't, Thou and thy Mother ne'er had fall'n to this.

Gil. His Father sure was seeking of the Lard when he was got.

Enter L. Fleetwood, her Train born up.

Crom. Where is this perjur'd Slave, thy Wittal Lord? Dares he not shew his Face, his guilty Face, Before the Person he has thus betray'd?

L. Fleet. Madam, I hope you mistake my honour'd Lord Lambert, I believe he designs the Throne for my dear Lord.

Crom. Fond Girl, because he has the Art of fawning, Dissembling to the height, can sooth and smile, Profess, and sometimes weep:— No, he'll betray him, as he did thy Brother; Richard the Fourth was thus deluded by him. No, let him swear and promise what he will, They are but steps to his own ambitious End; And only makes the Fool, thy credulous Husband, A silly deluded Property.

Enter Fleetwood.

Fleet. My honour'd Mother, I am glad to find you here; I hope we shall reconcile things between ye. Verily we should live in Brotherly Love together; come, ingeniously, you shall be Friends, my Lady Mother.

Crom. Curse on th' occasion of thy being a Kin to me.

Fleet. Why, an please ye, forsooth, Madam?

Crom. My Daughter had a Husband, Worthy the Title of my Son—in—Law; Ireton, my best of Sons: he'd Wit and Courage, And with his Counsels, rais'd our House to Honours, Which thy impolitick Easiness pulls down: And whilst you should be gaining Crowns and Kingdoms, Art poorly couzening of the World with fruitless Prayers.

Fleet. Nay, I'll warrant you, Madam, when there is any gadly Mischief to be done, I am as forward as the best; but 'tis good to take the Lard along with us in every thing. I profess ingeniously, as I am an honest Man, verily— ne'er stir— I shall act as becomes a good Christian.

Crom. A good Coxcomb. Do'st thou not see her reverend Highness there, That Minion now assumes that glorious Title I once, and my Son Richard's Wife enjoy'd, Whilst I am call'd the Night—mare of the Commonwealth? But wou'd I were, I'd so hag—ride the perjur'd Slaves, Who took so many Oaths of true Allegiance To my great Husband first, then to Richard— Who, whilst they reign'd, were most illustrious, Most high and mighty Princes; whilst fawning Poets

Write Panegyricks on 'em; and yet no sooner was The wondrous Hero dead, but all his glorious Titles fell to Monster of Mankind, Murderer Of Piety, Traytor to Heaven and Goodness.

Fleet. Who calls him so? Pray take their Names down: I profess ingeniously, forsooth, Madam, verily I'll order 'em, as I am here I will.

Crom. Thou, alas! they scorn so poor a thing as thou.

Fleet. Do they ingeniously? I'll be even with 'em, forsooth, Mother, as I am here I will, and there's an end on't.

Crom. I wou'd there were an end of our Disgrace and Shame, Which is but just begun, I fear. What will become of that fair Monument Thy careful Father did erect for thee, [To L. Fleetwood. Yet whilst he liv'd, next to thy Husband Ireton, Lest none shou'd do it for thee after he were dead; The Malice of proud Lambert will destroy all.

Fleet. I profess, Madam, you mistake my good Lord Lambert, he's an honest Man, and fears the Lard; he tells me I am to be the Man; verily he does, after all's done.

Cram. Yes, after all's done, thou art the Man to be pointed at.

Fleet. Nay, ingeniously, I scorn the Words, so I do: I know the great Work of Salvation to the Nation is to be wrought by me, verily.

Crom. Do, cant on, till Heaven drop Kingdoms in thy Mouth: Dull, silly Sot, thou Ruin of our Interest; thou fond, incorrigible, easy Fool.

Enter Page.

Page. My Lord, the Committee of Safety waits your coming.

Fleet. Why, law you now, forsooth— I profess verily, you are ingeniously the hardest of Belief— tell the Honourable Lords I'm coming: Go, Lady–mother, go home with my Wife; and verily you'll see things go to your wish— I must to Coach.

L. Fleet. Madam, your humble Servant. [To La. Lam.

Fleet. Honour'd Lady, I kiss your Hands.

[Exeunt Crom. Fleet, and L. Fleet.

Enter Loveless.

Lov. Was this the thing that is to be Protector? This little sniveling Fellow rule three Kingdoms? But leave we Politicks, and fall to Love, Who deals more Joys in one kind happy moment Than Ages of dull Empire can produce.

L. Lam. Oh Gods! shall I who never yielded yet, But to him to whom three Kingdoms fell a Sacrifice, Surrender at first Parley?

Lov. Perhaps that Lover made ye gayer Presents, But cou'd not render you a Heart all Love, Or Mind embyass'd in Affairs of Blood. —I bring no Guilt to fright you from my Embraces, But all our Hours shall be serene and soft.

L. Lam. Ah, Gilliflower, thy Aid, or I am lost; Shall it be said of me in after Ages, When my Fame amongst Queens shall be recorded, That I, ah Heavens! regardless of my Country's Cause, Espous'd the wicked Party of its Enemies, The Heathenish Heroicks? ah, defend me!

Lov. Nay— by all that's—

L. Lam. Ah, hold! Do not profane my Ears with Oaths or Execrations, I cannot bear the Sound.

Lov. Nay, nay— by Heav'n I'll not depart your Lodgings, till that soft Love that plays so in your Eyes give me a better Proof— by—

L. Lam. Oh hold, I die, if you proceed in this Abomination.

Lov. Why do you force me to't? d'ye think to put me off with such a Face— such Lips— such Smiles— such Eyes, and every Charm— You've made me mad, and I shall swear my Soul away, if disappointed now.

Gil. Ah, save the Gentleman's Soul, I beseech ye, Madam.

L. Lam. I'm much inclin'd to Acts of Piety— And you have such a Power, that howe'er I incommode my Honour— [Leaning on him, smiling. He goes to lead her out, Enter La. Desbro. —Desbro here! How unseasonably she comes?

L. Des. Cry mercy, Madam, I'll withdraw a while.

L. Lam. Ah, Desbro! thou art come in the most lucky Minute— I was just on the point of falling— As thou say'st, these Heroicks have the strangest Power—

L. Des. I never knew a Woman cou'd resist 'em.

L. Lam. No marvel then, our Husbands use 'em so, betray 'em, banish 'em, sequester, murder 'em, and every way disarm 'em—

L. Des. But their Eyes, Madam.

L. Lam. Ay, their Eyes, Desbro; I wonder our Lords shou'd take away their Swords, and let 'em wear their Eyes.

L. Des. I'll move it to the Committee of Safety, Madam, those Weapons should be taken from 'em too.

L. Lam. Still they'll have some to be reveng'd on us.

L. Des. Ay, so they will will; My Lord says, a Cavalier is a kind of Hydra, knock him o'th' Head as often as you will, he has still one to peep up withal.

Enter Page.

Page. Madam, here's Mr. Freeman to speak with your Honour.

Lov. That's a Friend of mine, Madam, and 'twou'd be unnecessary he saw your Highness and I together: let us withdraw—

L. Lam. Withdraw! why, what will Desbro say?

L. Des. O Madam, I know your Virtue and your Piety too well to suspect your Honour wrongfully: 'tis impossible a Lady that goes to a Conventicle twice a Day, besides long Prayers and loud Psalm— singing, shou'd do any thing with an Heroick against her Honour. Your known Sanctity preserves you from Scandal— But here's Freeman— [Puts 'em in.

Enter Freeman.

Free. So, Madam— you are very kind—

L. Des. My charming Freeman, this tedious Day of Absence has been an Age in love. How hast thou liv'd without me?

Free. Like one condemn'd, sad and disconsolate, And all the while you made your Husband happy.

L. Des. Name not the Beastly Hypocrite, thou know'st I made no other use of him, But a dull Property to advance our Love.

Free. And 'tis but Justice, Maria, he sequester'd me of my whole Estate, because, he said, I took up Arms in Ireland, on Noble Ormond's Side; nay, hir'd Rogues, perjur'd Villains— Witnesses with a Pox, to swear it too; when at that time I was but Eight Years Old; but I escap'd as well as all the Gentry and Nobility of England. To add to this, he takes my Mistress too.

L. Des. You mistake, my lovely Freeman; I married only thy Estate, the best Composition I cou'd make for thee, and I will pay it back with Interest too.

Free. You wou'd suspect my Love then, and swear that all the Adoration I pay you, were, as we do to Heav'n, for Interest only.

L. Des. How you mistake my Love, but do so still, so you will let me give these— Proofs of it. [Gives him Gold.

Free. Thus, like Atlante, you drop Gold in my Pursuit To Love, I may not over–take you: What's this to giving me one happy minute? Take back your Gold, and give me current Love, The Treasure of your Heart, not of your Purse— When shall we meet, Maria?

L. Des. You know my leisure Hours are when my Honourable Lord is busied in Affairs of State, or at his Prayers; from which long–winded Exercise I have of late withdrawn my self: three Hours by the Clock he prays extemporary, which is, for National and Household Blessings: For the first— 'tis to confound the Interest of the King, that the Lard wou'd deliver him, his Friends, Adherers and Allies, wheresoever scatter'd about the Face of the whole Earth, into the Clutches of the Righteous: Press 'em, good Lard, even as the Vintager doth the Grape in the Wine–Press, till the Waters and gliding Channels are made red with the Blood of the Wicked. [In a Tone.

Free. And grant the Faithful to be mighty, and to be strong in Persecution; and more especially, ah! I beseech thee confound that malignant Tory Freeman— that he may never rise up in judgment against thy Servant, who has taken from him his Estate, his Sustenance and Bread; give him Grace of thy infinite Mercy, to hang himself, if thy People can find no zealous Witnesses to swear him to the Gallows legally. Ah, we have done very much for thee, Lard, thou shoud'st consider us thy Flock, and we shou'd be as good to thee in another thing. [In a Tone.

L. Des. Thou hit'st the zealous Twang right; sure thou hast been acquainted with some of 'em.

Free. Damn 'em, no; what honest Man wou'd keep 'em Company, where harmless Wit and Mirth's a Sin, laughing scandalous, and a merry Glass Abomination?

L. Des. Yes, if you drink Healths, my wicked Brother: otherwise, to be silently drunk, to be as abusive and satirical as you please, upon the Heroicks, is allowable— for laughing, 'tis not indeed so well; but the precise Sneer and Grin is lawful; no swearing indeed, but lying and dissimulation in abundance. I'll assure you, they drink as deep, and entertain themselves as well with this silent way of leud Debauchery, as you with all your Wit and Mirth, your Healths of the Royal Family.

Free. Nay, I confess, 'tis a great Pleasure to cheat the World.

L. Des. 'Tis Power, as divine Hobbes calls it.

Free. But what's all this to Love? Where shall we meet anon?

L. Des. I'll tell you, what will please you as well— Your Friend is within with her Highness that shall be, if the Devil and her Husband's Politicks agree about the matter.

Free. Ha, has my cautious Railer manag'd matters so slyly?

L. Des. No, no, the matter was manag'd to his Hand; you see how Heav'n brings things about, for the Good of your Party; this Business will be worth to him at least a thousand Pound a year, or two, well manag'd— But see, my Lady's Woman.

Gil. Oh, Madam, my Lord— [Running cross the Stage into her Lady's Chamber.

Free. Death, how shall I bring my Friend off? he'll certainly be ruin'd.

Enter Gill. Lov. and Lady Lam.

Gill. Madam, he's coming up.

Lov. Madam, for my self I care not, but am much concern'd for you. [L. Lam. takes two Papers out of her Pocket, and gives 'em to Lov. and Free.

L. Lam. Here take these two Petitions, each of you one— Poor Fellows— you may be gone, your Petitions will not be granted.

Enter Lambert.

Lam. How now, my Dear, what Petitions?— Friends, what's your Bus'ness?

L. Lam. 'Tis enough we know their Business, Love, we are sufficient to dispatch such Suiters, I hope.

Lam. Pardon me, my Dear, I thought no harm; but I saw you frown, and that made me concern'd.

L. Lam. Frown! 'Twou'd make any Body frown, to hear the Impudence of Gentlemen, these Cavaliers— wou'd you think it, my Dear, if this Fellow has not the Impudence to petition for the Thirds of his Estate again, so justly taken from him for bearing Arms for the Man?—

L. Des. Nay, I'm inform'd, that they, but two Nights ago, in a Tavern, drunk a Health to the Man too.

Lam. How durst you, Sirrah, approach my Lady with any such saucy Address? you have receiv'd our Answer.

Lov. Death, I have scarce Patience. [Aside.

Free. We knew, my Lord, the Influence your Ladies have over you, and Women are more tender and compassionate naturally than Men; and, Sir, 'tis hard for Gentlemen to starve.

L. Lam. Have you not able Limbs? can ye not work?

Lov. Persons of our Education work!

Lam. Starve or beg then.

L. Lam. Education! why, I'll warrant there was that young Creature they call the Duke of Glocester, was as well educated as any Lad in the Parish; and yet you see he should have been bound Prentice to a Handy–Crafts Trade, but that our Lords could not spare Money to bind him out, and so they sent him to beg beyond Sea.

Lov. Death, I shall do Mischief: not all the Joy she gave me but now, can atone for this Blasphemy against the Royal Youth. [Aside.

Free. Patience— Well, my Lord, we find you are obdurate, and we'll withdraw.

Lam. Do so: And if you dare presume to trouble us any more, I'll have you whip'd, d'ye hear.

L. Des. Madam, I'll take my leave of your Ladyship.

[Ex. Lov. Free. and L. Des.

L. Lam. My Lord, 'twas I that ought to threaten 'em— but you're so forward still— what makes you from the Committee?

Lam. I left some Papers behind.

L. Lam. And they'll make use of your Absence to set up Fleetwood King.

Lam. I'll warrant ye, my Dear.

L. Lam. You'll warrant! you are a Fool, and a Coxcomb; I see I must go my self, there will be no Bus'ness done till I thunder 'em together: They want Old Oliver amongst 'em, his Arbitrary Nod cou'd make ye all tremble; when he wanted Power or Money, he need but cock in Parliament, and lay his Hand upon his Sword, and cry, I must have Money, and had it, or kick'd ye all out of Doors: And you are all mealy mouth'd, you cannot cock for a Kingdom.

Lam. I'll warrant ye, Dear, I can do as good a thing for a Kingdom.

L. Lam. You can do nothing as you shou'd do't: You want Old Oliver's Brains, Old Oliver's Courage, and Old Oliver's Counsel: Ah, what a politick Fellow was little Sir Anthony! What a

Head–piece was there! What a plaguy Fellow Old Thurlo, and the rest! But get ye back, and return me Protector at least, or never hope for Peace again.

Lam. My Soul, trouble not thy self, go in— With mine no Power can equal be, And I will be a King to humour thee. [Exeunt.

ACT III

SCENE I. A Council–Chamber, great Table, Chairs, and Papers.

Enter two Clerks, who lay Papers in Order, and Doorkeeper.

Door. Come, haste, haste, the Lords are coming— keep back there, room for the Lords, room for the honourable Lords: Heav'n bless your Worships Honours.

Enter Lambert, Fleetwood, Whitlock, Wariston, discoursing earnestly; to them Duckenfield, Cobbet, Hewson, Desbro, and others; Duck. takes Wariston by the Hand, and talks to him.

War. Bread a gued, Gentlemen, I's serv'd the Commonwealth long and faithfully; I's turn'd and turn'd to aud Interest and aud Religions that turn'd up Trump, and wons a me, but I's get naught but Bagery by my Sol; I's noo put in for a Pansion as well as rest o ya Loones.

Cob. What we can serve you in, my Lord, you may command.

Duc. And I too, my Lord, when the Government is new moulded.

War. Wons, Sirs, and I's sa moold it, 'twas ne'er sa moolded sen the Dam boon'd the Head on't.

Duc. I know there are some ambitious Persons that are for a single Person; but we'll have hot Work e'er we yield to that.

War. The faud Diel take 'em then for Archibald; 'tis warse than Monarchy.

Duc. A thousand times: have we with such Industry been pulling down Kings of the Royal Family, to set up Tyrants of our own, of mean and obscure Birth? No, if we're for a single Person, I'm for a lawful one.

War. Wons and ya have spoken aud, my Lord, so am I.

Due. But Lambert has a busy, haughty Spirit, and thinks to carry it; but we'll have no single Person.

War. Nor I, ods Bread; the faud Diel brest the Wem of Lambert, or any single Person in England. I's for yare Interest, my gued Lords. [Bowing.

Lam. My Lord Wariston, will you please to assume the Chair?

Enter Loveless, Freeman, and others with Petitions.

War. Ah, my gued Loord, I's yare most obedient humble Servant. [Bowing to Lam. all set.

41

All. Hum, hum.

Fleet. My Lords and Gentlemen, we are here met together in the Name of the Lard—

Duc. Yea, and I hope we shall hang together as one Man— A Pox upon your Preaching. [Aside.

Fleet. —And hope this Day's great Work will be for his Praise and Glory.

Duc. 'Bating long Graces, my Lord, we are met together for the Bus'ness of the Nation, to settle it, and to establish a Government.

Fleet. Yea, verily: and I hope you will all unanimously agree, it shall be your unworthy Servant.

Lam. What else, my Lord.

Fleet. And as thou, Lard, hast put the Sword into my Hand—

Due. So put it into your Heart— my Lord, to do Justice.

Fleet. Amen.

Due. I'd rather see it there than in your Hand— [Aside.

Fleet. For we are, as it were, a Body without a Head; or, to speak more learnedly, an Animal inanimate.

Hew. My Lord, let us use, as little as we can, the Language of the Beast, hard Words; none of your Eloquence, it savoureth of Monarchy.

Lam. My Lord, you must give Men of Quality leave to speak in a Language more gentile and courtly than the ordinary sort of Mankind.

Hew. My Lord, I am sorry to hear there are any of Quality among this honourable Dissembly. [Stands up.

Cob. Assembly, my Lord—

Hew. Well, you know my meaning; or if there be any such, I'm sorry they should own themselves of Quality.

Due. How! own themselves Gentlemen! Death, Sir, d'ye think we were all born Coblers?

Hew. Or if you were not, the more the pity, for little England, I say. [In a heat.

Fleet. Verily, my Lords, Brethren should not fall out, it is a Scandal to the good Cause, and maketh the wicked rejoice.

War. Wons, and theys garr the loosey Proverb on't te, when loons gang together by th' luggs, gued men get their ene.

All. He, he, he.

Due. He calls you Knaves by Craft, my Lords.

War. Bread a gued, take't among ye, Gentlemen, I's ment weel.

Fleet. I profess, my Lord Wariston, you make my Hair stand an end to hear how you swear.

War. Wons, my Loord, I's swear as little as your Lordship, only I's swear out, and ye swallow aud.

Due. There's a Bone for you to pick, my Lord.

All. He, he, he.

Lam. We give my Lord Wariston leave to jest.

Des. But what's this to the Government all this while? A dad I shall sit so late, I shall have no time to visit my Horses, therefore proceed to the Point.

Hew. Ay, to the Point, my Lords; the Gentleman that spoke last spoke well.

Cob. Well said, Brother, I see you will in time speak properly.

Duc. But to the Government, my Lords! [Beats the Table.

Lam. Put 'em off of this Discourse, my Lord. [Aside to War.

Des. My Lord Wariston, move it, you are Speaker.

War. The Diel a me, Sirs, and noo ya talk of a Speaker, I's tell ye a blithe Tale.

Fleet. Ingeniously, my Lord, you are to blame to swear so.

Lam. Your Story, my Lord.

War. By my Sol, mon, and there war a poor Woman the other Day, begg'd o'th' Carle the Speaker, but he'd give her nought unless she'd let a Feart; wons at last a Feart she lat. Ay marry, quoth the Woman, noo my Rump has a Speaker te.

All. He, he, he.

Due. But to our Bus'ness——

Des. Bus'ness; ay, there's the thing, I've a World on't. I shou'd go and bespeak a Pair of Mittins and Shears for my Hedger and Shearer, a pair of Cards for my Thrasher, a Scythe for my Mower, and a Screen—Fan for my Lady—Wife, and many other things; my Head's full of Bus'ness. I cannot stay—

Whit. Fy, my Lord, will you neglect the bus'ness of the Day? We meet to oblige the Nation, and gratify our Friends.

Des. Nay, I'll do any thing, so I may rise time enough to see my Horses at Night.

Lav. Damn 'em, what stuff's here for a Council—Table?

Free. Where are our English Spirits, that can be govern'd by such Dogs as these?—

Lam. Clerk, read the Heads of what past at our last sitting.

War. In the first place, I must mind your Lordships tol consider those that have been gued Members in the Commonwealth.

Fleet. We shall not be backward to gratify any that have serv'd the Commonwealth.

Whit. There's Money enough; we have taxt the Nation high.

Due. Yes, if we knew where to find it: however, read.

Clerk reads.] To Walter Walton, Draper, six thousand nine hundred twenty nine Pounds six Shillings and five Pence, for Blacks for his Highness's Funeral.

Lam. For the Devil's; put it down for Oliver Cromwel's Funeral: We'll have no Record rise up in Judgment for such a Villain.

Lav. How live Asses kick the dead Lion! [Aside.

Due. Hark ye, my Lords, we sit here to reward Services done to the Commonwealth; let us consider whether this be a Service to the Commonwealth or not?

Lam. However, we will give him Paper for't.

Hews. Ay, let him get his Money when he can.

Lam. Paper's not so dear, and the Clerk's Pains will be rewarded.

War. Right, my gued Lord,'sbred, that Cromwel was th' faudest limmer Loon that ever cam into lour Country, the faud Diel has tane him by th' Luggs for robbing our Houses and Land.

Fleet. No swearing, my Lord.

War. Weel, weel, my Loord, I's larne to profess and lee as weel as best on ya.

Hews. That may bring you profit, my Lord— but, Clerk, proceed.

Clerk reads.] To Walter Frost, Treasurer of the Contingencies, twenty thousand Pounds. To Thurloe, Secretary to his Highness—

Duc. To old Noll.

Clerk reads.] —Old Noll, ten thousand Pounds, for unknown Service done the Commonwealth— To Mr. Hutchinson, Treasurer of the Navy, two hundred thousand Pounds—

War. Two hundred thousand Pound; Owns, what a Sum's there?— Marry it came from the Mouth of a Cannon sure.

Clerk reads.] A Present to the Right Honourable and truly Virtuous Lady, the Lady Lambert, for Service done to the late Protector—

Hews. Again— say Cromwel.

Clerk. —Cromwel— six thousand Pound in Jacobus's.

War. 'Sbread, sike a Sum wou'd make me honour the Face of aud Jemmy.

Clerk. To Mr. Ice six thousand Pound; to Mr. Loether, late Secretary to his High—

Whit. To Oliver Cromwel say, can you not obey Orders?

Clerk. —Secretary to Oliver Cromwel— two thousand nine hundred ninety nine Pounds for Intelligence and Information, and piously betraying the King's Liege People.

War. Haud, haud, Sirs, Mary en ya gift se fast ya'll gif aud away from poor Archibald Johnson.

Whit. Speak for your self, my Lord; or rather, my Lord, do you speak for him. [To Lam.

Lam. Do you move it for him, and I'll do as much for you anon. [Aside to Whit.

Whit. My Lord, since we are upon Gratifications,— let us consider the known Merit of the Lord Wariston, a Person of industrious Mischiefs to the malignant Party, and great Integrity to us, and the Commonwealth.

War. Gued faith, an I's ha been a trusty Trojon, Sir, what say you, may very gued and gracious Loords?—

Duc. I scorn to let a Dog go unrewarded; and you, Sir, fawn so prettily, 'tis pity you shou'd miss Preferment.

Hews. And so 'tis; come, come, my Lords, consider he was ever our Friend, and 'tis but reasonable we shou'd stitch up one another's broken Fortunes.

Duc. Nay, Sir, I'm not against it.

All. 'Tis Reason, 'tis Reason.

Free. Damn 'em, how they lavish out the Nation!

War. Scribe, pretha read my Paper.

Hews. Have you a Pertition there?

Cob. A Petition, my Lord.

Hews. Pshaw, you Scholards are so troublesome.

Lam. Read the Substance of it. [To the Clerk.

Clerk. That your Honours wou'd be pleas'd, in consideration of his Service, to grant to your Petitioner, a considerable Sum of Money for his present Supply.

Fleet. Verily, order him two thousand Pound—

War. Two thousand poond? Bread a gued, and I's gif my Voice for Fleetwood. [Aside.

Lam. Two thousand; nay, my Lords, let it be three.

War. Wons, I lee'd, I lee'd; I's keep my Voice for Lambert— Guds Benizon light on yar Sol, my gued Lord Lambert.

Hews. Three thousand Pound! why such a Sum wou'd buy half Scotland.

War. Wons, my Lord, ya look but blindly on't then: time was, a Mite on't had bought aud shoos in yar Stall, Brother, tho noo ya so abound in Irish and Bishops Lands.

Duc. You have nick'd him there, my Lord.

All. He, he, he.

War. Scribe— gang a tiny bit farther.

Clerk. —And that your Honours would be pleas'd to confer an Annual Pension on him—

Lam. Reason, I think; what say you, my Lords, of five hundred Pound a Year?

All. Agreed, agreed.

War. The Diel swallow me, my Lord, ya won my Heart.

Due. 'Tis very well— but out of what shall this be rais'd?

Lam. We'll look what Malignants' Estates are forfeit, undispos'd of— let me see— who has young Freeman's Estate?

Des. My Lord, that fell to me.

Lam. What all the fifteen hundred Pound a Year?

Des. A Dad, and all little enough.

Free. The Devil do him good with it.

Des. Had not the Lard put it into your Hearts to have given me two thousand per Annum out of Bishops Lands, and three thousand per Annum out of the Marquess's Estate; how shou'd I have liv'd and serv'd the Commonwealth as I have done?

Free. A plague confound his Honour, he makes a hard shift to live on Eight thousand Pound a Year, who was born and bred a Hedger.

Lov. Patience, Friend.

Lam. I have been thinking— but I'll find out a way.

Lov. Or betray some honest Gentleman, on purpose to gratify the Loone.

Lam. And, Gentlemen, I am bound in Honour and Conscience to speak in behalf of my Lord Whitlock; I think fit, if you agree with me, he shou'd be made Constable of Windsor Castle, Warden of the Forest, with the Rents, Perquisities, and Profits thereto belonging; nor can your Lordships confer a Place of greater Trust and Honour in more safe Hands.

Due. I find he wou'd oblige all to his side. [Aside. Has he not part of the Duke of Buckingham's Estate already, with Chelsey House, and several other Gifts?

Lam. He has dearly deserv'd 'em; he has serv'd our Interest well and faithfully.

Due. And he has been well paid for't.

Whit. And so were you, Sir, with several Lordships, and Bishops Lands, you were not born to, I conceive.

Duc. I have not got it, Sir, by knavish Querks in Law; a Sword that deals out Kingdoms to the brave, has cut out some small parcels of Earth for me. And what of this? [Stands up in a heat.

Whit. I think, Sir, he that talks well, and to th' purpose, may be as useful to the Commonwealth as he that fights well. Why do we keep so many else in Pension that ne'er drew Sword, but to talk, and rail at the malignant Party; to libel and defame 'em handsomly, with pious useful Lyes, Which pass for Gospel with the common Rabble, And edify more than Hugh Peter's Sermons; And make Fools bring more Grist to the publick Mill. Then, Sir, to wrest the Law to our convenience Is no small, inconsiderate Work.

Free. And which you may be hang'd for very shortly— [Aside.

Lam. 'Tis granted, my Lord, your Merit's infinite— We made him Keeper of the Great Seal, 'tis true, 'tis Honour, but no Salary.

Duc. Ten thousand Pound a Year in Bribes will do as well.

Lam. Bribes are not so frequent now as in Old Noll's Days.

Hews. Well, my Lord, let us be brief and tedious, as the saying is, and humour one another: I'm for Whitlock's Advance.

Lam. I move for a Salary, Gentlemen, Scobel and other petty Clerks have had a thousand a Year; my Lord sure merits more.

Hews. Why— let him have two thousand then.

Fleet. I profess ingeniously, with all my Heart.

Whit. I humbly thank your Lordships— but, if I may be so bold to ask, from whence shall I receive it?

Lam. Out of the Customs.

Cob. Brotherly Love ought to go along with us— but, under favour, when this is gone, where shall we raise new Supplies?

Lam. We'll tax the Nation high, the City higher, They are our Friends, our most obsequious Slaves, Our Dogs to fetch and carry, our very Asses—

Lov. And our Oxes, with the help of their Wives. [Aside.

Lam. Besides, the City's rich, and near her time, I hope, of being deliver'd.

War. Wons a gued, wad I'd the laying o' her, she shou'd be sweetly brought to Bed, by my Sol.

Des. The City cares for no Scotch Pipers, my Lord.

War. By my Sol, but she has danc'd after the gued Pipe of Reformation, when the Covenant Jigg gang'd maryly round, Sirs.

Clerk. My Lords, here are some poor malignant Petitioners.

Lam. Oh, turn 'em out, here's nothing for 'em; these Fellows were petitioning my Lady to day— I thought she had given you a satisfactory Answer,

Lov. She did indeed, my Lord: but 'tis a hard Case, to take away a Gentleman's Estate, without convicting him of any Crime.

Lam. Oh, Sir, we shall prove that hereafter.

Lov. But to make sure Work, you'll hang a Man first and examine his Offence afterwards; a Plague upon your Consciences: My Friend here had a little fairer Play; your Villains, your Witnesses in Pension swore him a Colonel for our glorious Master, of ever blessed Memory, at eight Years old; a Plague upon their Miracles.

Fleet. Ingeniously, Sirrah, you shall be pillory'd for defaming our reverend Witnesses: Guards, take 'em to your Custody both.

Free. Damn it, I shall miss my Assignation with Lady Desbro; a Pox of your unnecessary prating, what shall I do? [Guards take 'em away.

Lam. And now, my Lords, we have finished the Business of the Day. My good Lord Fleetwood, I am entirely yours, and at our next sitting shall approve my self your Creature—

Whit. My good Lord, I am your submissive Vassal.

War. Wons, my Lord, I scorn any Man shou'd be mere yare Vassal than Archibald Johnson. [To Fleetwood.

[Ex. All.

SCENE II. A Chamber in Lady Desbro's House.

Enter La. Desbro, and Corporal in haste.

L. Des. Seiz'd on, secur'd! Was there no time but this? What made him at the Committee, or when there why spoke he honest Truth? What shall I do, good Corporal? Advise; take Gold, and see if you can corrupt his Guards: but they are better paid for doing Mischief; yet try, their Consciences are large. [Gives him Gold.

Cor. I'll venture my Life in so good a Cause, Madam. [Exit.

Enter Tom.

Tom. Madam, here's Mr. Ananias Gogle, the Lay–Elder of Clement's Parish.

L. Des. Damn the sham Saint; am I now in Condition to be plagu'd with his impertinent Nonsense?

Tom. Oh! Pray, Madam, hear him preach a little; 'tis the purest Sport—

Enter Ananias.

Ana. Peace be in this Place.

L. Des. A blessed hearing; he preaches nothing in his Conventicles, but Blood and Slaughter. [Aside. What wou'd you, Sir? I'm something busy now.

Ana. Ah, the Children of the Elect have no Business but the great Work of Reformation: Yea verily, I say, all other Business is profane, and diabolical, and devilish; Yea, I say, these Dressings, Curls, and Shining Habilliments— which take so up your time, your precious time; I say, they are an Abomination, yea, an Abomination in the sight of the Righteous, and serve but as an Ignis fatuus, to lead vain Man astray— I say again— [Looking now and then behind on the Page.

L. Des. —You are a very Coxcomb.

Ana. I say again, that even I, upright I, one of the new Saints, find a sort of a— a— I know not what— a kind of a Motion as it were— a stirring up— as a Man may'say, to wickedness— Yea, verily it corrupteth the outward Man within me.

L. Des. Is this your Business, Sir, to rail against our Clothes, as if you intended to preach me into my Primitive Nakedness again?

Ana. Ah, the naked Truth is best; but, Madam, I have a little work of Grace to communicate unto you, please you to send your Page away—

L. Des. Withdraw— sure I can make my Party good with one wicked Elder:— Now, Sir, your Bus'ness. [Ex. Tom. —Be brief.

Ana. As brief as you please— but— who in the sight of so much Beau – – ty— can think of any Bus'ness but the Bus'ness— Ah! hide those tempting Breasts,— Alack, how smooth and warm they are— [Feeling 'em, and sneering.

L. Des. How now, have you forgot your Function?

Ana. Nay, but I am mortal Man also, and may fall seven times a day— Yea verily, I may fall seven times a day— Your Ladyship's Husband is old,— and where there is a good excuse for falling,— ah, there the fall— ing— is excusable.— And might I but fall with your Ladyship,— might I, I say.—

L. Des. How, this from you, the Head o' th' Church Militant, the very Pope of Presbytery?

Ana. Verily, the Sin lieth in the Scandal; therefore most of the discreet pious Ladies of the Age chuse us, upright Men, who make a Conscience of a Secret, the Laity being more regardless of their Fame.— In sober sadness, the Place— inviteth, the Creature tempting, and the Spirit very violent within me. [Takes and ruffles her.

L. Des. Who waits there?— I'm glad you have prov'd your self what I ever thought of all your pack of Knaves.

Ana. Ah, Madam! Do not ruin my Reputation; there are Ladies of high Degree in the Commonwealth, to whom we find our selves most comforting; why might not you be one?— for, alas, we are accounted as able Men in Ladies Chambers, as in our Pulpits: we serve both Functions—

Enter Servants.

Hah! her Servants— [Stands at a distance.

L. Des. Shou'd I tell this, I shou'd not find belief. [Aside.

Ana. Madam, I have another Errand to your Ladiship.— It is the Duty of my Occupation to catechize the Heads of every Family within my Diocese; and you must answer some few Questions I shall ask.— In the first place, Madam,— Who made ye?

L. Des. So, from Whoring, to a zealous Catechism— who made me? what Insolence is this, to ask me Questions which every Child that lisps out Words can answer!

Ana. 'Tis our Method, Madam.

L. Des. Your Impudence, Sirrah,— let me examine your Faith, who are so sawcy to take an account of mine— Who made you? But lest you shou'd not know, I will inform you: First, Heav'n made you a deform'd, ill–favour'd Creature; then the Rascal your Father made you a

51

Taylor; next, your Wife made you a Cuckold; and lastly the Devil has made you a Doctor; and so get you gone for a Fool and a Knave all over.

Ana. A Man of my Coat affronted thus!

L. Des. It shall be worse, Sirrah, my Husband shall know how kind you wou'd have been to him, because your Disciple and Benefactor, to have begot him a Babe of Grace for a Son and Heir.

Ana. Mistake not my pious meaning, most gracious Lady.

L. Des. I'll set you out in your Colours: Your impudent and bloody Principles, your Cheats, your Rogueries on honest Men, thro their kind, deluded Wives, whom you cant and goggle into a Belief, 'tis a great work of Grace to steal, and beggar their whole Families, to contribute to your Gormandizing, Lust and Laziness; Ye Locusts of the Land, preach Nonsense, Blasphemy, and Treason, till you sweat again, that the sanctify'd Sisters may rub you down, to comfort and console the Creature.

Ana. Ah! Am—

L. Des. Sirrah, be gone, and trouble me no more— be gone— yet stay— the Rogue may be of use to me— Amongst the heap of Vice, Hypocrisy, and Devils that possess all your Party, you may have some necessary Sin; I've known some honest, useful Villains amongst you, that will swear, profess, and lye devoutedly for the Good Old Cause.

Ana. Yea, verily, I hope there are many such, and I shou'd rejoice, yea, exceedingly rejoice in any Gadly Performance to your Ladiship.

L. Des. This is a pious Work: You are a Knave of Credit, a very Saint with the rascally Rabble, with whom your seditious Cant more prevails, your precious Hum and Ha, and gifted Nonsense, than all the Rhetorick of the Learn'd or Honest.

Ana. Hah!

L. Des. —In fine, I have use of your Talent at present, there's one now in Confinement of the Royal Party— his Name's Freeman.

Ana. And your Ladiship wou'd have him dispatch'd; I conceive ye— but wou'd you have him dispatch'd privately, or by Form of Law? we've Tools for all uses, and 'tis a pious Work, and meritorious.

L. Des. Right, I wou'd indeed have him dispatch'd, and privately; but 'tis hither privately, hither to my Chamber, privately, for I have private Bus'ness with him. D'ye start?— this must be done— for you can pimp I'm sure upon occasion, you've Tools for all uses; come, resolve, or I'll discover your bloody Offer. Is your Stomach so queasy it cannot digest Pimping, that can swallow Whoring, false Oaths, Sequestration, Robbery, Rapes, and Murders daily?

Ana. Verily, you mistake my pious Meaning; it is the Malignant I stick at; the Person, not the Office: and in sadness, Madam, it goeth against my tender Conscience to do any good to one of the Wicked.

L. Des. It must stretch at this time; go haste to the Guard, and demand him in my Husband's Name; here's something worth your Pains— having releas'd him, bring him to me, you understand me— go bid him be diligent, and as you behave your self, find my Favour; for know, Sir, I am as great a Hypocrite as you, and know the Cheats of your Religion too; and since we know one another, 'tis like we shall be true.

Ana. But shou'd the Man be missing, and I call'd to account?—

L. Des. He shall be return'd in an hour: go, get you gone, and bring him, or— no more— [*Ex.*
Ana. For all degrees of Vices, you must grant, There is no Rogue like your Geneva Saint.
[*Exeunt.*

ACT IV

SCENE I. A Chamber in La. Desbro's House. Candles, and Lights.

Enter L. Desbro and Freeman.

L. Des. By what strange Miracle, my dearest Freeman, wert thou set at liberty?

Free. On the zealous Parole of Rabbie Ananias; that Rhetorick that can convert whole Congregations of well–meaning Blockheads to errant Knaves, has now mollify'd my Keeper; I'm to be render'd back within this Hour: let's not, my dear Maria, lose the precious minutes this Reverend Hypocrite has given us.

L. Des. Oh! you are very gay, have you forgot whose Prisoner you are, and that perhaps, e'er many Days are ended, they may hang you for High–Treason against the Commonwealth? they never want a good thorow–stitch'd Witness to do a Murder lawfully.

Free. No matter, then I shall die with Joy, Maria, when I consider, that you lov'd so well to give me the last Proof on't.

L. Des. Are you in earnest, Freeman? and wou'd you take what Honour will not suffer me to grant?

Free. With all my Heart, Honour's a poor Excuse. Your Heart and Vows (your better part) are mine; you've only lent your Body out to one whom you call Husband, and whom Heaven has mark'd for Cuckoldom. Nay, 'tis an Act of honest Loyalty, so to revenge our Cause; whilst you were only mine, my honest Love thought it a Sin to press these Favours from you; 'twas injuring my self as well as thee; but now we only give and take our Right.

L. Des. No more, my Husband's old—

Free. Right, my dear Maria, and therefore—

L. Des. —May possibly die—

Free. He will be hang'd first.

L. Des. —I hope so— either of which will do our Bus'ness— unreasonable Freeman, not to have Patience till my Husband be hang'd a little.

Free. But what if Destiny put the Change upon us, and I be hang'd instead of Desbro?

L. Des. Why then thou art not the first gallant Fellow that has died in the Good and Royal Cause; and a small taste of Happiness will but turn thee off the Ladder with the sadder Heart.

Free. Hast thou the Conscience, lovely as thou art, To deal out all thy Beauty to a Traitor? Is not this Treason of the highest Nature, To rob the Royal Party of such Treasure, And give it to our mortal Enemies? For Shame, be wise, and just, And do not live a Rebel to our Cause; 'Tis Sin enough to have Society with such a wicked Race.

L. Des. But I am married to him.

Free. So much the worse, to make a League and Covenant with such Villains, and keep the sinful Contract; a little harmless Lying and Dissimulation I'll allow thee, but to be right down honest, 'tis the Devil.

L. Des. This will not do, it never shall be said I've been so much debauch'd by Conventicling to turn a sainted Sinner; No, I'm true to my Allegiance still, true to my King and Honour. Suspect my Loyalty when I lose my Virtue: a little time, I'm sure, will give me honestly into thy Arms; if thou hast Bravery, shew it in thy Love.

Free. You will o'ercome, and shame me every way;— but when will this Change come? and till it do, what Pawn will you give me, I shall be happy then?

L. Des. My Honour, and that Happiness you long for, and take but two Months time for their Redemption.

Free. How greedily I'll seize the Forfeiture!

L. Des. But what am I like to get if this Change do come?

Free. A Slave, and whatever you please to make of him.

L. Des. Who knows, in such an universal Change, how you may alter too?

Free. I'll give ye Bond and Vows, unkind Maria,— Here take my Hand— Be it known unto all Men, by these Presents, that I, John Freeman of London, Gent, acknowledge my self in Debt to Maria Desbro, the Sum of one Heart, with an incurable Wound; one Soul, destin'd hers from its first Being; and one Body, whole, sound, and in perfect Health; which I here promise to pay to the said Maria, upon Demand, if the aforesaid John Freeman be not hang'd before such Demand made. Whereto I set my Hand— and seal it with my Lips. [In a Tone.

L. Des. And I, in consideration of such Debt, do freely give unto the abovesaid John Freeman, the Heart and Body of the abovesaid Maria Desbro, with all Appurtenances thereto belonging, whenever it shall please Heaven to bring my Husband fairly to the Gallows. [In a Tone.

Free. Amen— kiss the Book— [Kisses her.

[Ana. hums without.

L. Des. Hah! that's Ananias; sure some Danger's near, the necessary Rascal gives us notice of.

Free. 'Tis so, what wouldst thou have me do?

L. Des. Thou art undone if seen— here, step within this Curtain. [He goes.

Enter Ananias, humming, and spreading his Cloak wide; Desbro behind him, puffing in a Chafe.

Des. Ads nigs, what a Change is here like to be?— puff, puff— we have manag'd Matters sweetly— to let the Scotch General undermine us; puff, puff.

L. Des. What's the Matter?

Des. Nothing, Cockey, nothing, but that we are like to return to our first nothing.

Ana. Yea, verily, when our time's come; but ah, the great Work of Reformation is not yet fully accomplish'd, which must be wrought by the Saints, and we cannot spare one of them until the Work be finish'd.

Des. Yea, yea, it is finish'd I doubt, puff, puff: fie, fie, what a Change is here!

Ana. Patience, ah, 'tis a precious Virtue!—

Des. Patience, Sir! what, when I shall lose so many fine Estates which did appertain to the Wicked; and which, I trusted, had been establish'd ours, and tell'st thou me of Patience? puff, puff. [Walking fast.

Ana. How! lose 'em, Sir? handle the matter with Patience; I hope the Committee of Safety, or the Rump, will not do an illegal thing to one of the Brethren.

Des. No, no, I have been a trusty Knave to them, and so I have found them all to me: but Monk! Monk! O that ever we should be such blind Fools to trust an honest General!

Ana. Patience, Sir! what of him?

Des. I just now receiv'd private Intelligence, he's coming out of Scotland with his Forces— puff, puff.

Ana. Why, let him come a Gad's Name, we have those will give him a civil Salute, if he mean not honourably to the Commonwealth. Patience, Sir.

Des. But if he proves the stronger, and shou'd chance to be so great a Traitor to us, to bring in the Man— the King.

L. Des. How, the King, Husband! the great Heroick!

Free. Death, this Woman is a Sybil: ah, noble Monk!

Ana. Hum— the King!—

Des. Ah, and with the King, the Bishops; and then, where's all our Church and Bishops Lands! oh, undone— puff, puff.

Ana. How, bring in the King and Bishops! my righteous Spirit is raised too— I say, I will excommunicate him for one of the Wicked, yea, for a profane Heroick, a Malignant, a Tory,— a— I say, we will surround him, and confound him with a mighty Host; yea, and fight the Lard's Battel with him: yea, we will—

Des. Truckle to his Pow'r— puff, puff.

Ana. Nay, I say verily, nay; for, in Sadness, I will die in my Calling.

Des. So I doubt shall I— which is Ploughing, Hedging, and Ditching.

Ana. Yea, we have the Sword of the Righteous in our Hand, and we will defend the mighty Revenues of the Church, which the Lard hath given unto his People, and chosen ones— I say, we will defend—

Des. Ah, Patience, Sir, ah, 'tis a pious Virtue—

Ana. Ah, it is Zeal in one of us, the Out—goings of the Spirit.

Enter Tom.

Tom. Sir, will you go down to Prayers? the Chaplain waits.

Des. No, no, Boy, I am too serious for that Exercise, I cannot now dissemble, Heav'n forgive me.

Ana. How, Sir, not dissemble— ah, then you have lost a great Virtue indeed, a very great Virtue; ah, let us not give away the Good Old Cause— but, as we have hitherto maintain'd it by gadly Cozenage, and pious Frauds, let us persevere— ah, let us persevere to the end; let us not lose our Heritage for a Mess of Pottage, that is, let us not lose the Cause for Dissimulation and Hypocrisy, those two main Engines that have earned on the great Work.

Des. Verily, you have prevail'd, and I will go take counsel of my Pillow: Boy— call my Man to undress me— I'll to Bed, for I am sick at Heart. [Ex. Tom.

Free. Death, what shall I do now?

[Des. walks, she whispers Ana.

L. Des. You must get my Man off, or we're undone.

Ana. Madam, be comforted, Heaven will bring all things about for our Advantage— [As Des. turns.

L. Des. But he's behind the Curtains, Man—

[Des. turns from 'em.

Ana. Ah, let Providence alone— [Spreads his Cloak wide, and goes by degrees toward the Bed.] —Your pious Lady, Sir, is doubtful, but I will give her ample Satisfaction.

Des. Ah, do, Mr. Ananias, do, for she's a good and virtuous Lady, certo she is.

[Ana. goes close to the Bed–post, and speaks over his Shoulder.

Ana. Get ye behind my Cloak—

L. Des. Indeed, Sir, your Counsel and Assistance is very comfortable.

Ana. We should be Help–meets to one another, Madam.

Des. Alack, good Man!

[L. Des. goes to coax her Husband.

L. Des. Ay, my dear, I am so much oblig'd to him, that I know not, without thy Aid, how to make him amends.

Free. So, this is the first Cloak of Zeal I ever made use of.

[Ana. going, spreading his Cloak, to the Door; Free. behind goes out.

Des. Good Lady, give him his twenty pieces, adad, he worthily deserves 'em. [Gives her Gold.

L. Des. Indeed, and so he does, Dear, if thou knew'st all.— What say you now, do I not improve in Hypocrisy? And shall I not in time make a precious Member of your Church? [To Ana.

Ana. Verily, your Ladyship is most ingenious and expert.— Sir, I most humbly take my leave. [Ex. Ana.

Enter Tom.

Tom. My Lord, my Lord Lambert has sent in all haste for you, you must attend at his House immediately.

Des. So, he has heard the News— I must away— let my Coach be ready. [Ex. Des.

L. Des. How unlucky was this that Freeman should be gone— Sirrah, run and see to o'ertake him, and bring him back. [Exeunt.

SCENE II. A fine Chamber in La. Lambert's House.

Enter Gilliflower and Loveless by dark, richly drest.

Lov. Where am I, Gilliflower?

Gill. In my Lady's Apartment, Sir, she'll be with you presently; you need not fear betraying, Sir, for I'll assure you I'm an Heroick in my Heart: my Husband was a Captain for his Majesty of ever–blessed Memory, and kill'd at Naseby, God be thanked, Sir.

Lov. What pity 'tis that thou shouldst serve this Party?

Gill. Bating her Principles, my Lady has good Nature enough to oblige a Servant; and truly, Sir, my Vails were good in old Oliver's Days; I got well by that Amour between him and my Lady; the man was lavish enough.

Lov. Yes, of the Nation's Treasure— but prithee tell me, is not thy Lady mad, raving on Crowns and Kingdoms?

Gill. It appears so to you, who are not us'd to the Vanity of the Party, but they are all so mad in their Degree, and in the Fit they talk of nothing else, Sir: we have tomorrow a Hearing as they call it.

Lov. What's that, a Conventicle?

Gill. No, no, Sir, Ladies of the last Edition, that present their Grievances to the Council of Ladies, of which my Lady's chief, which Grievances are laid open to the Committee of Safety, and so redress'd or slighted, as they are.

Lov. That must be worth one's Curiosity, could one but see't.

Gill. We admit no Man, Sir.

Lov. 'Sdeath, for so good a sight I will turn Woman, I'll act it to a hair.

Gill. That would be excellent.

Lov. Nay, I must do't; the Novelty is rare— but I'm impatient— prithee let thy Lady know I wait.

Gill. She's in Affairs of State, but will be here immediately; mean time, retire into her Cabinet, I'll send the Page with Lights, there you may repose till my Lady comes, on the Pallat. [She leads him out.

SCENE III. A great Chamber of State, and Canopy in Lambert's House.

And at a Table, seated Lambert, Fleetwood, Desbro, Hewson, Duckenfield, Wariston, Cobbet; all half drunk, with Bottles and Glasses on the Table; L. Lam. and L. Fleet.

Lam. My Lord Wariston, you are not merry to night.

War. Wons, Mon, this Monk sticks in my Gullet, the muckle Diel pull him out by th' Lugs; the faud Loone will en spoyle and our Sport, mon.

Lam. I thought I had enough satisfied all your Fears; the Army's mine, that is,— 'tis yours, my Lords, and I'll imploy it too so well for the Good of the Commonwealth, you shall have Cause to commend both my Courage and Conduct; my Lord Wariston, will you accompany me?

War. Ah, my gued Lord, the Honour is too great. 'Tis not but I's dare fight, my Lord, but I love not the limmer Loone, he has a villanous honest Face an's ene; I's ken'd him ence, and lik't him not; but I's drink tol yar gued Fortune; let it gang aboote, ene and ad, Sirs. [All drink.

Lam. We'll leave all Discourse of Bus'ness, and give our selves to Mirth; I fancy good Success from this day's Omen.

Enters Gill, whispers L. Lam. she rises.

L. Lam. Waited so long!

Gill. And grew impatient, an't please your Highness; must I go tell him you cannot see him to night.

L. Lam. Not for the World; my silly Politician will be Busying himself in the dull Affairs of State; —Dull in comparison of Love, I mean; I never lov'd before; old Oliver I suffer'd for my Interest, And 'tis some Greatness, to be Mistress to the best; But this mighty Pleasure comes a propos, To sweeten all the heavy Toils of Empire.

Gill. So it does, an't please your Highness.

L. Lam. Go, let him know I'm coming— Madam, I must beg your Pardon; you hear, my Lord to morrow goes on his great Expedition; and, for any thing we know, may fall a glorious Sacrifice to the Commonwealth; therefore 'tis meet I offer up some Prayers for his Safety, and all my leisure Hours 'twixt this and that, will be too few— Your humble Servant, Madam. [Ex. L. Lam. and Gill.

L. Fleet. My Dear, I'll leave you too, my time of Devotion is come, and Heav'n will stay for no Body; where are my People? is my Coach ready, or my Chair?

Fleet. Go in your Chair, my Love, lest you catch cold.

L. Fleet. And light your Flambeaus,— I love to have my Chair surrounded with Flambeaus.

Enter Page.

Page. Your Chair is ready, Madam.

[She goes out led by Fleet.

Hews. What think ye now, my Lords, of settling the Nation a little? I find my Head swim with Politicks, and what ye call ums.

War. Wons, and wad ya settle the Nation when we real our selves?

Hews. Who, pox, shall we stand making Childrens Shoes all the Year? No, no, let's begin to settle the Nation, I say, and go thro—stitch with our Work.

Duc. Right, we have no Head to obey; so that if this Scotch General do come whilst we Dogs fight for the Bone, he runs away with it.

Hews. Shaw, we shall patch up matters with the Scotch General, I'll warrant you: However, here's to our next Head— One and all. [All drink.

Fleet. Verily, Sirs, this Health—drinking savoureth of Monarchy, and is a Type of Malignancy.

War. Bread, my Lord, no preaching o'er yar Liquer, wee's now for a Cup o' th' Creature.

Cob. In a gadly way you may; it is lawful.

Lam. Come, come, we're dull, give us some Musick— come, my Lord, I'll give you a Song, I love Musick as I do a Drum, there's Life and Soul in't, call my Musick.

Fleet. Yea, I am for any Musick, except an Organ.

War. Sbread, Sirs, and I's for a Horn—pipe, I've a faud Theefe here shall dance ye Dance tol a Horn—pipe, with any States—man a ya aud.

All. He, he, he.

Duc. I know not what your faud Theefe can do; but I'll hold you a Wager, Colonel Hewson, and Colonel Desbro shall dance ye the Seint's Jigg with any Sinner of your Kirk, or field Conventicler.

War. Wons, and I's catch 'em at that Sport, I's dance tol 'em for a Scotch Poond; but farst yar Song, my Lord, I hope 'tis boody, or else 'tis not werth a Feart.

All. He, he, he.

SONG, sung by my Lord Lambert.

_A Pox of the States–man that's witty,

That watches and plots all the sleepless Night,

For seditious Harangues to the Whigs of the City,

And piously turns a Traitor in spite.

Let him wrack, and torment his lean Carrion,

To bring his sham–Plots about,

Till Religion, King, Bishop, and Baron,

For the publick Good, be quite routed out._

_Whilst we that are no Politicians,

But Rogues that are resolute, bare–fac'd and great,

Boldly head the rude Rabble in open Sedition,

Bearing all down before us in Church and in State.

Your Impudence is the best State—trick,

And he that by Law means to rule,

Let his History with ours be related,

Tho we prove the Knaves, 'tis he is the Fool._

War. The Diel a me, wele sung, my Lord, and gen aud Trades fail, yas make a quaint Minstrel.

All. He, he, he.

War. Noo, Sirs, yar Dance? [They fling Cushions at one another, and grin. Musick plays.] — Marry, Sirs, an this be yar dancing, tol dance and ne'er stir Stap, the Diel lead the Donce for Archibald.

[When they have flung Cushions thus a while to the Musick time, they beat each other from the Table, one by one, and fall into a godly Dance; after a while, Wariston rises, and dances ridiculously a while amongst them; then to the Time of the Tune, they take out the rest, as at the Cushion—Dance, or in that nature. Wariston being the last taken in, leads the rest.

—Haud, Minstrels, haud; Bread a gued. I's fatch ad Ladies in— lead away, Minstrels, tol my Lady's Apartment.

[Musick playing before all.

[Exeunt dancing.

SCENE IV. Flat.

Enter Page.

Page. Cock, Here must I wait, to give my Lady notice when my Lord approaches;— The fine Gentleman that is alone with her, gave me these two fine Pieces of Gold, and bad me buy a Sword to fight for the King withal; and I'm resolv'd to lay it all out in a Sword, not a penny in Nickers, and fight for the Heroicks as long as I have a Limb, if they be all such fine Men as this within. But hark, sure I hear some coming.— [Exit.

[Flat Scene draws off, discovers L. Lam. on a Couch, with Loveless, tying a rich Diamond—Bracelet about his Arm: a Table behind with Lights, on which a Velvet Cushion, with a Crown and Scepter cover'd.

Lov. This Present's too magnificent: such Bracelets young Monarchs shou'd put on.

L. Lam. Persons like me, when they make Presents, Sir, must do it for their Glory, not considering the Merit of the Wearer: yet this, my charming Loveless, comes short of what I ought to pay thy Worth; comes short too of my Love.

Lov. You bless me, Madam—

L. Lam. This the great Monarch of the World once ty'd about my Arm, and bad me wear it, till some greater Man shou'd chance to win my Heart; Thou art that Man whom Love has rais'd above him; Whom every Grace and every Charm thou hast Conspire to make thee mightier to my Soul; And Oliver, illustrious Oliver, Was yet far short of thee.

Lov. He was the Monarch then whose Spoils I triumph in.

L. Lam. They were design'd too for Trophies to the young and gay. Ah, Loveless! that I cou'd reward thy Youth With something that might make thee more than Man, As well as to give the best of Women to thee— [Rises, takes him by the Hand, leads him to the Table. He starts. — Behold this gay, this wondrous glorious thing.

Lov. Hah— a Crown— and Scepter! Have I been all this while So near the sacred Relicks of my King; And found no awful Motion in my Blood, Nothing that mov'd sacred Devotion in me? [Kneels. —Hail sacred Emblem of great Majesty, Thou that hast circled more Divinity Than the great Zodiack that surrounds the World. I ne'er was blest with sight of thee till now, But in much reverenc'd Pictures— [Rises and bows.

L. Lam. Is't not a lovely thing?

Lov. There's such Divinity i' th' very Form on't, Had I been conscious I'd been near the Temple, Where this bright Relick of the glorious Martyr Had been enshrin'd, 't had spoil'd my soft Devotion. —'Tis Sacrilege to dally where it is; A rude, a saucy Treason to approach it With an unbended Knee: for Heav'ns sake, Madam, Let us not be profane in our Delights, Either withdraw, or hide that glorious Object.

L. Lam. Thou art a Fool, the very sight of this— Raises my Pleasure higher: Methinks I give a Queen into thy Arms, And where I love I cannot give enough; [Softly. —Wou'd I cou'd set it on thy Head for ever, 'Twou'd not become my simple Lord The thousandth part so well. [Goes to put it on his Head, he puts it back.

Lov. Forbear, and do not play with holy things; Let us retire, and love as Mortals shou'd, Not imitate the Gods, and spoil our Joys.

L. Lam. Lovely, and unambitious! What hopes have I of all your promis'd Constancy, Whilst this which possibly e'er long may adorn my Brow, And ought to raise me higher in your Love, Ought to transform you even to Adoration, Shall poorly make you vanish from its Lustre? Methinks the very Fancy of a Queen Is worth a thousand Mistresses of less illustrious Rank.

Lov. What, every pageant Queen? you might from thence infer I'd fall in love with every little Actress, because She acts the Queen for half an hour, But then the gaudy Robe is laid aside.

L. Lam. I'll pardon the Comparison in you.

Lov. I do not doubt your Power of being a Queen, But trust, it will not last. How truly brave would your great Husband be, If, whilst he may, he paid this mighty Debt To the right Owner! If, whilst he has the Army in his Power, He made a true and lawful use of it, To settle our great Master in his Throne; And by an Act so glorious raise his Name Even above the Title of a King.

L. Lam. You love me not, that would persuade me from My Glory.

Enter Gilliflower.

Gill. Oh, Madam, the Lords are all got merry, as they call it, and are all dancing hither.

L. Lam. What, at their Oliverian Frolicks?— Dear Loveless, withdraw, I wou'd not give the fond believing Fool a Jealousy of me.

Gill. Withdraw, Madam? 'tis impossible, he must run just into their Mouths.

L. Lam. I'm ill at these Intrigues, being us'd to Lovers that still came with such Authority, that modestly my Husband wou'd withdraw— but Loveless is in danger, therefore take care he be not seen.

Gill. Heav'ns! they are coming, there's no Retreat—

L. Lam. Lie down on the Couch— and cover him you with the Foot–Carpet— So, give me my Prayer–Book.

[He lies down along on the Couch, they cover him with the Carpet: L. Lam. takes her Book, sits down on his Feet, and leans on the Back of the Couch reading; Gill. stands at t'other end, they enter dancing as before.

—What Insolence is this? do you not hear me, you— Sots— whom Gaiety and Dancing do so ill become.

War. [Singing.] Welcome, Joan Sanderson, welcome, welcome. [Goes to take her out, she strikes him. Wons, Madam, that's no part o' th' Dance.

L. Lam. No, but 'tis part of a reward for your Insolence, Which possibly your Head shall answer for—

65

Lam. Pardon him, my Dear, he meant no Disrespect to thee.

L. Lam. How dare you interrupt my Devotion, Sirrah? Be gone with all your filthy ill–bred Crew.

[Lam. sits down on Lov.

Lam. My only Dear, be patient; hah!— Something moves under me; Treason, Treason! [He rises.

[Lov. rolls off, and turns Lam. over, the rest of the Men run out crying Treason, Treason, overthrowing the Lights, putting 'em out.

L. Lam. Treason, Treason! my Lord, my Lord!

Lam. Lights there, a Plot, a Popish Plot, Lights!

L. Lam. The Crown, the Crown, guard the Crown! [She groping about, finds Lov. by his Clothes, knows him. —Here, take this Key, the next room is my Bed–chamber, Secure yourself a moment.— [Ex. Loveless. Lights there, the Crown— who art thou? [Takes hold of Lam.

Lam. 'Tis I.

L. Lam. Ah, my Lord, what's the matter?—

Lam. Nay, my Lady, I ask you what's the matter?

Enter Page with Lights.

By Heaven, all is not well; hark ye, my fine she Politician, who was it you had hid beneath this Carpet?

L. Lam. Heav'ns! dost hear him, Gilliflower? Sure the Fellow's mad.

Gill. Alack, my Lord, are you out of your honourable Wits? Heav'n knows, my Lady was at her Devotion.

Lam. Baud, come, confess thy self to be one. At her Devotion! yes, with a He Saint.

Gill. Ah! Gad forbid the Saints should be so wicked.

L. Lam. Hark ye, thou little sniveling Hypocrite, who hast no Virtue but a little Conduct in Martial Discipline; who hast by Perjuries, Cheats, and pious Villanies, wound thy self up into the Rabble's Favour, where thou mayst stand till some more great in Roguery remove thee from that height, or to the Gallows, if the King return: hast thou the Impudence to charge my Virtue?

Lam. I know not, Madam, whether that Virtue you boast were lost, or only stak't, and ready for the Gamester; but I am sure a Man was hid under this Carpet.

L. Lam. Oh Heav'ns, a Man!

Gill. Lord, a Man! Are you sure 'twas a Man, my Lord?—— Some villanous Malignant, I'll warrant.

Lam. It may be so.

Gill. Alack, the Wickedness of these Heroicks to hide under Carpets; why they'l have the impudence to hide under our Petticoats shortly, if your Highness take 'em not down. [To Lady Lam.

Lam. I do believe so; Death— a Cuckold? shall that black Cloud shade all my rising Fame?

L. Lam. Cuckold! Why, is that Name so great a Stranger to ye, Or has your rising Fame made ye forget How long that Cloud has hung upon your Brow? —'Twas once the height of your Ambition, Sir; When you were a poor–sneaking Slave to Cromwell, Then you cou'd cringe, and sneer, and hold the Door, And give him every Opportunity, Had not my Piety defeated your Endeavours.

Lam. That was for Glory, Who wou'd not be a Cuckold to be great? —If Cromwell leap'd into my Saddle once, I'll step into his Throne for't: but, to be pointed at By Rascals that I— rule— 'tis insupportable.

L. Lam. How got this Fellow drunk? call up my Officers! Who durst deliver him this quantity of Wine? Send strait in my Name, to summon all the Drunken Committee of Safety into my Presence. By Heav'n, I'll show you, Sir— yes they shall See what a fine King they're like to have In Honest, Gadly, Sober, Wise Jack Lambert. —Nay, I'll do't; d'ye think to take away my Honour thus? I, who by my sole Politicks and Management Have set you up, Villain of Villains, Sirrah. —Away— summon 'em all. [To Gilliflower.

Lam. Stay— be not so rash; who was beneath the Carpet?

L. Lam. I will not answer thee.

Lam. Nor any living thing?

L. Lam. No Creature in the Room, thou silly Ideot, but Gilliflower and I— at our Devotion, praying to Heav'n for your Success to morrow— and am I thus rewarded? [Weeps, Gill. weeps too.

Lam. My Soul, I cannot bear the Sight of Tears From these dear Charming Eyes.

L. Lam. No matter, Sir, the Committee shall right me.

Lam. Upon my Knees I ask thy Pardon, Dear; by all that's good, I wou'd have sworn I'd felt something stir beneath me as I sat, which threw me over.

L. Lam. Only your Brains turn'd round with too much drinking and dancing, Exercises you are not us'd to— go sleep, and settle 'em, for I'll not deign to Bed with you to night— retire, as e'er you hope to have my Aid in your Advancement to the Crown.

Lam. I'm gone— and once more pardon my Mistake. [Bows, and goes out. Ex. Gill.

L. Lam. —So, this fighting Fool, so worshipp'd by the Rabble, How meanly can a Woman make him sneak?— The happy Night's our own— [To Loveless.

Enter Gill. Loveless.

Lov. Excellent Creature, how I do adore thee!

L. Lam. But you, perhaps, are satisfied already—

Lov. Never; shou'dst thou be kind to all Eternity. Thou hast one Virtue more, I pay thee Homage for; I heard from the Alcove how great a Mistress thou art in the dear Mystery of Jilting.

L. Lam. That's the first Lesson Women learn in Conventicles, Religion teaches those Maxims to our Sex: by this Kings are deposed, and Commonwealths are rul'd; By Jilting all the Universe is fool'd. [Exeunt.

ACT V

SCENE I. A Street.

Enter Corporal, half drest; with Soldiers, Joyner, and Felt—maker.

Cor. Ha, Rogues, the City—Boys are up in Arms; brave Boys, all for the King now!

Felt. Have a care what you say, Sir; but as to the City's being in Mutiny, that makes well for us: we shall fall to our old Trade of plundering; something will fall to the Righteous, and there is Plunder enough.

Cor. You plunder, Sirrah! knock him down, and carry him into the Guard—room, and secure him.

[Two Soldiers seize him.

1 Sold. They say the Committee of Safety sate all Night at General Lambert's, about some great Affair— some rare Change, Rogues.

2 Sold. Yes, and to put off Sorrow, they say, were all right reverendly drunk too.

Cor. I suppose there is some heavenly matter in hand; there was Treason cried out at the General's last night, and the Committee of no Safety all ran away.

1 Sold. Or rather reel'd away.

Cor. The Ladies squeak'd, the Lords fled, and all the House was up in Arms.

Felt. Yea, and with Reason they say; for the Pope in disguise was found under the Lady's Bed, and two huge Jesuits as big as the tall Irish—man, with Blunderbusses; having, as 'tis said, a Design to steal the Crown, now in Custody of the General—

2 Sold. Good lack, is't possible?

Joyn. Nay, Sir, 'tis true, and is't not time we look'd about us?

Cor. A Pox upon ye all for lying Knaves— secure 'em both on the Guard till farther Order— and let us into th' City, Boys: hay for Lombard—Street.

2 Sold. Ay, hay for Lombard—Street; there's a Shop I have mark'd out for my own already.

1 Sold. There's a handsom Citizen's Wife, that I have an Eye upon, her Husband's a rich Banker, I'll take t'one with t'other.

Joyn. You are mistaken, Sir, that Plunder is reserv'd for us, if they begin to mutiny; that wicked City that is so weary of a Commonwealth.

2 Sold. Yes, they're afraid of the Monster they themselves have made.

Enter Lov. and Free. in disguise.

Cor. Hah, my noble Colonel! what, in disguise!

Free. We have made our Escapes— and hope to see better times shortly, the noble Scotch General is come, Boys.

Enter Captain of the Prentices, and a great Gang with him, arm'd with Swords, Staffs, etc.

Capt. Come, my Lads, since you have made me Captain, I'll lead you bravely on; I'll die in the Cause, or bring you off with Victory.

1 Pren. Here's a Club shall do some Execution: I'll beat out Hewson's t'other Eye; I scorn to take him on the blind side.

Capt. In the first Place, we must all sign a Petition to my Lord Mayor.—

2 Pren. Petitions! we'll have no Petition, Captain; we are for Club–Law, Captain.

Capt. Obey, or I leave you.

All. Obey, Obey.

Capt. Look ye, we'll petition for an honest Free Parliament I say.

1 Pren. No Parliament, no Parliament, we have had too much of that Mischief already, Captain.

All. No Parliament, no Parliament.

Capt. Farewel, Gentlemen, I thought I might have been heard.

Free. Death, Sirs, you shall hear the Captain out.

All. We obey, we obey.

Capt. I say an honest Free Parliament, not one pick'd and chosen by Faction; but such an one as shall do our Bus'ness, Lads, and bring in the Great Heroick.

All. Ay, ay, the Great Heroick, the Great Heroick.

Lov. A fine Youth, and shou'd be encourag'd.

Capt. Good— in the next Place, the noble Scotch General is come, and we'll side with him.

Free. Ay, ay, all side with him.

1 Pren. Your Reason, Captain, for we have acted too much without Reason already.

2 Pren. Are we sure of him, Captain?

Capt. Oh, he'll doubtless declare for the King, Boys.

All. Hay, Viva le Roy, viva le Monk!

Capt. Next, I hear there's a Proclamation coming out to dissolve the Committee of no Safety.

All. Good, good.

Capt. And I hope you are all brave enough to stand to your Loyal Principles with your Lives and Fortunes.

All. We'll die for the Royal Interest.

Capt. In the next Place, there's another Proclamation come out.

2 Pren. This Captain is a Man of rare Intelligence; but for what, Captain?

Capt. Why— to— hang us all, if we do not immediately depart to our respective Vocations: How like you that, my Lads?

2 Pren. Hum— hang'd! I'll e'en home again.

1 Pren. And I too, I do not like this hanging.

2 Pren. A Man looks but scurvily with his Neck awry.

3 Pren. Ay, ay, we'll home.

Capt. Why, now you shew what precious Men you are— the King wou'd be finely hop'd up with such Rascals, that for fear of a little hanging would desert his Cause; a Pox upon you all, I here discharge ye— —Take back your Coward Hands and give me Hearts. [Flings 'em a Scroll. I scorn to fight with such mean–spirited Rogues; I did but try your boasted Courages.

Lov. Brave Boy.

Lov. and Free. We'll die with thee, Captain—

All. Oh, noble Captain, we recant—

1 Pren. We recant, dear Captain, we'll die, one and all.

All. One and all, one and all.

Capt. Why, so there's some trusting to you now.

3 Pren. But is there such a Proclamation, Captain?

Capt. There is; but anon, when the Crop–ear'd Sheriff begins to read it, let every Man enlarge his Voice, and cry, no Proclamation, no Proclamation.

All. Agreed, agreed.

Lov. Brave noble Lads, hold still your Resolution, And when your leisure Hours will give ye leave, Drink the King's Health, here's Gold for you to do so.

Free. Take my Mite too, brave Lads. [Gives 'em Gold.

All. Hay! Viva the brave Heroicks!

Enter Ananias Gogle.

Ana. Hum, what have we here, a Street–Conventicle— or a Mutiny? Yea, verily, it is a Mutiny— What meaneth this Appearance in hostile manner, in open Street, by Day–light?

Capt. Hah! one of the sanctify'd Lay Elders, one of the Fiends of the Nation, that go about like roaring Lions seeking whom they may devour.

Lov. Who, Mr. Ananias the Padder?

Ana. Bear witness, Gentlemen all, he calls me Highway–man; thou shalt be hang'd for Scandal on the Brethren.

Lov. I'll prove what I say, Sirrah; do you not rob on the High–way i' th' Pulpit? rob the Sisters, and preach it lawful for them to rob their Husbands; rob Men even of their Consciences and Honesty; nay rather than stand out, rob poor Wenches of their Bodkins and Thimbles?

Ana. I commit ye; here, Soldiers, I charge ye in the Name of— of— marry, I know not who, in my Name, and the good People of England, take 'em to safe Custody.

Capt. How, lay hold of honest Gentlemen! Noble Cavaliers, knock him down.

All. Knock him down, knock him down.

Free. Hold, worthy Youths; the Rascal has done me Service.

Ana. [Pulling off his Hat to 'em all.] Ye look like Citizens, that evil Spirit is entered in unto you, oh Men of London! that ye have changed your Note, like Birds of evil Omen; that you go astray after new Lights, or rather no Lights, and commit Whoredom with your Fathers Idols, even in the midst of the Holy City, which the Saints have prepared for the Elect, the Chosen ones.

Capt. Hark ye, Sirrah, leave preaching, and fall to declaring for us, or thou art mortal.

Ana. Nay, I say nay, I will die in my Calling— yea, I will fall a Sacrifice to the Good Old Cause; abomination ye with a mighty Hand, and will destroy, demolish and confound your Idols, those heathenish Malignants whom you follow, even with Thunder and Lightning, even as a Field of Corn blasted by a strong Blast.

Lov. Knock him down!

All. Down with Dagon, down with him!

Enter Hewson with Guards.

Hews. Ah, Rogues, have I caught ye napping? [They all surround him and his Red–Coats.

All. Whoop Cobler, Whoop Cobler!

[The Boys, Lov. and Free. Corp. and Sold. beat off Hewson and his Party. Ana. gets a Sword, and fights too.

SCENE II. Changes to a Chamber in La. Lambert's House.

Enter L. Lam. and Gill.

Gill. I've had no time to ask your Highness how you slept to Night; but that's a needless Question.

L. Lam. How mean you? do you suspect my Virtue? do you believe Loveless dares attempt any thing against my Honour? No, Gilliflower, he acted all things so like a Gentleman, that every moment takes my Heart more absolutely.

Gill. My Lord departed highly satisfied.

L. Lam. She is not worthy of Intrigues of Love, that cannot manage a silly Husband as she pleases— but, Gilliflower, you forget that this is Council day.

Gill. No, but I do not, Madam, some important Suitors wait already.

Enter L. Des. and L. Fleetwood.

L. Lam. Your Servant, Madam Desbro, thou'rt welcome— Gilliflower, are all things ready in the Council–Chamber? We that are great must sometimes stoop to Acts, That have at least some shew of Charity; We must redress the Grievance of our People.

L. Fleet. She speaks as she were Queen, but I shall put a spoke in her rising Wheel of Fortune, or my Lord's Politicks fail him.

[Scene draws off, Table with Papers: Chairs round it.

L. Lam. Where are the Ladies of the Council?— how remiss they are in their Attendance on us.

L. Fleet. Us! Heav'ns, I can scarce endure this Insolence!— We will take care to mind 'em of their Duty—

L. Lam. We, poor Creature! how simply Majesty becomes her? [They all sitting down, enter L. Cromwel angrily, and takes her Place, L. Lam. uppermost. —Madam, as I take it, at our last sitting, our Pleasure was, that you shou'd sit no more.

Crom. Your Pleasure! Is that the General Voice? This is my Place in spite of thee, and all thy fawning Faction, and I shall keep it, when thou perhaps, shalt be an humble Suppliant here at my Foot–stool.

L. Lam. I smile at thee.

Cram. Do, and cringe; 'tis thy business to make thee popular. But 'tis not that— Nor thy false Beauty that will serve thy Ends.

L. Lam. Rail on; declining Majesty may be excus'd, Call in the Women that attend for redress of Grievances.

[Ex. Page.

Enter Page with Women, and Loveless dress'd as a Woman.

Gentlewomen, what's your Bus'ness with us?

Lov. Gentlewomen! some of us are Ladies.

L. Lam. Ladies in good time; by what Authority, and from whom do you derive your Title of Ladies?

L. Fleet. Have a care how you usurp what is not your own!

Lov. How the Devil rebukes Sin! [Aside.

L. Des. From whom had you your Honours, Women?

Lov. From our Husbands.

Gill. Husbands, who are they, and of what standing?

2 Lady. Of no long standing, I confess.

Gill. That's a common Grievance indeed.

L. Des. And ought to be redress'd.

L. Lam. And that shall be taken into consideration; write it down, Gilliflower; who made your Husband a Knight, Woman?

Lov. Oliver the first, an't please ye.

L. Lam. Of horrid Memory; write that down— who yours?

2 Lady. Richard the fourth, an't like your Honour.

Gill. Of sottish Memory; shall I write that down too?

L. Des. Most remarkably.

Crom. Heav'ns! Can I hear this Profanation of our Royal Family? [Aside.

L. Lam. I wonder with what impudence Noll and Dick cou'd Knightify your Husbands; for 'tis a Rule in Heraldry, that none can make a Knight but him that is one; 'tis Sancha Pancha's Case in Don Quixot.

Crom. How dare you question my Husband's Authority? [Rises in Anger. Who nobly won his Honour in the Field, Not like thy sneaking Lord who gain'd his Title From his Wife's gay Love-tricks— Bartering her Honour for his Coronet.

L. Lam. Thou ly'st, my Husband earn'd it with his Sword, Braver and juster than thy bold Usurper, Who waded to his Glory through a Sea Of Royal Blood—

L. Des. Sure Loveless has done good on her, and converted her.

L. Fleet. Madam, I humbly beg you will be patient, you'll ruin all my Lord's Designs else— Women, proceed to your Grievances, both publick and private.

Lov. I petition for a Pension; my Husband, deceas'd, was a constant active man, in all the late Rebellion, against the Man; he plunder'd my Lord Capel, he betray'd his dearest Friend Brown

Bushel, who trusted his Life in his Hands, and several others; plundering their Wives and Children even to their Smocks.

L. Lam. Most considerable Service, and ought to be consider'd.

2 Lady. And most remarkably, at the Trial of the late Man, I spit in's Face, and betray'd the Earl of Holland to the Parliament.

Crom. In the King's Face, you mean— it shew'd your Zeal for the Good Cause.

2 Lady. And 'twas my Husband that headed the Rabble, to pull down Gog and Magog, the Bishops, broke the Idols in the Windows, and turn'd the Churches into Stables and Dens of Thieves; rob'd the Altar of the Cathedral of the twelve pieces of Plate call'd the twelve Apostles, turn'd eleven of 'em into Money, and kept Judas for his own use at home.

L. Fleet. On my Word, most wisely perform'd, note it down—

3 Lady. And my Husband made Libels on the Man from the first Troubles to this day, defam'd and profan'd the Woman and her Children, printed all the Man's Letters to the Woman with Burlesque Marginal Notes, pull'd down the sumptuous Shrines in Churches, and with the golden and Popish Spoils adorn'd his own Houses and Chimney–Pieces.

L. Lam. We shall consider these great Services.

Lov. To what a height is Impudence arriv'd? [Aside.

L. Lam. Proceed to private Grievances.

Lov. An't please your Honours, my Husband prays too much; which both hinders his private bus'ness at home, and his publick Services to the Commonwealth—

L. Lam. A double Grievance— set it down, Gilliflower.

Lov. And then he rails against the Whore of Babylon, and all my neighbours think he calls me Whore.

Cram. A most unpardonable fault.

L. Lam. We'll have that rectify'd, it will concern us.

Lov. Then he never kisses me, but he says a long Grace, which is more mortifying than inviting.

L. Des. That is the fault of all the new Saints, which is the reason their Wives take a pious care, as much as in them lies, to send 'em to Heaven, by making 'em Cuckolds.

L. Fleet. A very charitable Work, and ought to be encourag'd.

[Loveless gives in a Petition to Gilliflower.

Gill. The humble Petition of the Lady Make–shift. [Reads. ——Heav'ns, Madam, here are many thousand Hands to't of the distressed Sex.

All. Read it.

Gill. Reads.] Whereas there pass'd an Act, June 24th, against Fornication and Adultery, to the great detriment of most of the young Ladies, Gentlewomen, and Commonalty of England, and to the utter decay of many whole Families, especially when married to old Men; your Petitioners most humbly beg your Honours will take this great Grievance into mature Consideration, and the said Act may be repealed. ——A Blessing on 'em, they shall have my Hand too.

L. Lam. We acknowledge, there are many Grievances in that Act; but there are many Conveniences too, for it ties up the villanous Tongues of Men from boasting our Favours.

Crom. But as it lays a Scandal on Society— tis troublesome, Society being the very Life of a Republick— Peters the first, and Martin the second.

Lov. But in a Free–State, why shou'd we not be free?

L. Des. Why not? we stand for the Liberty and Property of our Sex, and will present it to the Committee of Safety.

Lov. Secondly, we desire the Heroicks, vulgarly call'd the Malignant, may not be look'd on as Monsters, for assuredly they are Men; and that it may not be charg'd to us as a Crime to keep 'em company, for they are honest Men.

2 Lady. And some of 'em Men that will stand to their Principles.

L. Lam. Is there no other honest Men that will do as well?

3 Lady. Good Men are scarce.

L. Lam. They're all for Heroicks, sure 'tis the mode to love 'em— I cannot blame 'em. [Aside.

Lov. And that when we go to Morning and Evening Lectures, to Tantlings, or elsewhere, and either before or after visit a private Friend, it may be actionable for the wicked to scandalize us, by terming of it, abusing the Creature, when 'tis harmless recreating the Creature.

All. Reason, Reason.

Lov. Nor that any Husband shou'd interrupt his Wife, when at her private Devotion.

Enter Page.

L. Lam. I have been too late sensible of that Grievance.

Gill. And, Madam, I wou'd humbly pray a Patent for Scolding, to ease my Spleen.

Page. An please your Highness, here's a Messenger arriv'd Post with Letters from my Lord the General.

[Ex. Page.

L. Lam. Greater Affairs— oblige us to break up the Council. [Rises, the Women retire.

Enter Page with Messenger, or Letters.

—What means this haste? [Opens, and reads 'em.

Crom. Hah, bless my Eye–sight, she looks pale,— now red again; some turn to his Confusion, Heav'n, I beseech thee.

L. Lam. My Lord's undone! his Army has deserted him; Left him defenceless to the Enemies Pow'r. Ah, Coward Traytors! Where's that brutal Courage, That made you so successful in your Villanies? Has Hell, that taught you Valour, now abandon'd ye? —How in an instant are my Glories fall'n!

Crom. Ha, ha, ha — What, has your Highness any Cause of Grief?

Gill. Call up your Courage, Madam, do not let these things scoff you— you may be yet a Queen: Remember what Lilly told you, Madam.

L. Lam. Damn Lilly, who with lying Prophecies has rais'd me to the hopes of Majesty: a Legion of his Devils take him for't.

Crom. Oh, have a care of Cursing, Madam.

L. Lam. Screech–Owl, away, thy Voice is ominous. Oh I cou'd rave! but that it is not great; — And silent Sorrow— has most Majesty.

Enter Wariston, huffing.

War. Wons, Madam, undone, undone; our honourable Committee is gone to th' Diel, and the damn'd loosey Rump is aud in aud; the muckle Diel set it i'solt, and his Dam drink most for't.

Crom. The Committee dissolv'd! whose wise work was that? it looks like Fleetwood's silly Politicks.

War. Marry, and yar Ladiship's i'th' right,'twas en the Work o'th' faud Loone, the Diel brest his Wem for't.

Enter Hewson, Desbro, Whitlock, Duc. and Cob.

Hew. So, Brethren in Iniquity, we have spun a fine Thred, the Rump's all in all now, rules the Roast, and has sent for the General with Scissers and Rasor.

Whit. With a Sisseraro, you mean.

Hew. None of your Terms in Law, good Brother.

War. Right; but gen ya have any Querks in Law, Mr. Lyar, that will save our Crags, 'twill be warth a Fee.

Duc. We have plaid our Cards fair.

War. I's deny that; Wans, Sirs, ya plaid 'em faul; a Fule had the shooftling of'em, and the Muckle Diel himself turn up Trump.

Whit. We are lost, Gentlemen, utterly lost; who the Devil wou'd have thought of a Dissolution?

Hews. Is there no Remedy?

Duc. Death, I'll to the Scotch General; turn but in time as many greater Rogues than I have done, and 'twill save my Stake yet— Farewel, Gentlemen.

Des. No Remedy?

War. Nene, Sirs, again the King's Evil; Bread, Sirs, ya's ene gan tol yar Stall agen: I's en follow Duckenfield— Farewel, Mr. Leyer.

L. Lam. See the Vicissitudes of human Glory. These Rascals, that but yesterday petition'd me With humble Adoration, now scarce pay Common Civilities due to my Sex alone.

Enter Fleetwood.

Crom. How now, Fool, what is't that makes ye look so pertly? Some mighty Business you have done, I'll warrant.

Fleet. Verily, Lady Mother, you are the strangest Body; a Man cannot please you— Have I not finely circumvented Lambert? made the Rump Head, who have committed him to the Tower; ne'er stir now that I have, and I'm the greatest Man in England, as I live I am, as a Man may say.

Crom. Yes, till a greater come. Ah, Fool of Fools, not to fore–see the danger of that nasty Rump.

L. Fleet. Good Madam, treat my Lord with more Respect.

Crom. Away, fond Fool, born with so little Sense, To doat on such a wretched Idiot; It was thy Fate in Ireton's days to love him, Or you were foully scandalized.

Fleet. You are not so well spoken of neither, ne'er stir now, and you go to that. I can be King to morrow if I will.

Crom. Thou lyest, thou wo't be hang'd first; mark that I tell thee so. I'll prove Cassandra to thee, and prophesy thy Doom; Heav'n pays the Traitor back with equal Measure. Remember how you serv'd my poor Son Richard.

[Ex. Crom. and Page.

Fleet. She's mad— Come, my Dear, let's leave the House of this Villain, that meant to have cozen'd me illegally or three Kingdoms— but that I outwitted him at last. [Ex. Fleet. L. Fleet, and Page.

Enter Page.

L. Lam. Imprison'd too, i'th' Tower! what Fate is mine? [Leans on Des.

Page. Madam, the fine Heroick's come to wait on you.

L. Lam. Hah! Loveless! let him not see the Ruin of my Greatness, which he foretold, and kindly begg'd I wou'd usurp no more. [Weep.

Enter Loveless.

Lov. This News has brought me back, I love this Woman, Vain as she is, in spite of all her Fopperies of State— [Bows to her, and looks sad.

L. Lam. Alas, I do not merit thy Respect, I'm fall'n to Scorn, to Pity and Contempt. [Weeping. Ah, Loveless, fly the wretched— Thy Virtue is too noble to be shin'd on By any thing but rising Suns alone: I'm a declining Shade—

Lov. By Heaven, you were never great till now; I never thought thee so much worth my Love, My Knee, and Adoration, till this Minute. [Kneels. —I come to offer you my Life, and all The little Fortune the rude Herd has left me.

L. Lam. Is there such God–like Virtue in your Sex? Or, rather, in your Party. Curse on the Lyes and Cheats of Conventicles, That taught me first to think Heroicks Devils, Blood–thirsty, leud, tyrannick, salvage Monsters. —But I believe 'em Angels all, if all like Loveless. What heavenly thing then must the Master be, Whose Servants are divine?

[Enter Page running.

Page. Oh, Madam! all the Heroick Boys are up in Arms, and swear they'll have your Highness, dead or alive,— they have besieg'd the House.

L. Lam. Heav'ns, the Rabble!— those faithless things that us'd to croud my Coach's Wheels, and stop my Passage, with their officious Noise and Adoration.

Enter Freeman.

Free. Loveless, thy Aid; the City–Sparks are up; Their zealous Loyalty admits no Bounds. A glorious Change is coming, and I'll appear now barefac'd.

Lov. Madam, fear not the Rabble; retire. Freeman and I can still 'em. Leads her in, and bows low.

Free. My dear Maria, I shall claim ye shortly—

L. Des. Do your worst, I'm ready for the Challenge. [Go in.

[Ex. Lov. and Free. another way.

SCENE III. The Street.

Enter Captain and the rest.

Capt. I say we'll have the She–Politican out, she did more mischief than her Husband, pitiful, dittiful Lambert; who is, thanks be prais'd, in the Tower, to which place Lord of his Mercy bring all the King's Enemies.

All. Amen, Amen.

Enter Lov. and Freeman.

Lov. Why, how now, Captain, what, besiege the Women! No, let us lead our Force to nobler Enemies.

Capt. Nay, noble Chief, your Word's our Law.

Lov. No, I resign that Title to the brave Scotch General, who has just now enter'd the City.

Capt. We know it, Sir; do you not observe how the Crop–ear'd Fanaticks trot out of Town?— The Rogues began their old belov'd Mutiny, but 'twould not do.

Lov. A Pox upon 'em, they went out like the Snuff of a Candle, stinkingly and blinkingly.

1 Pr. Ay, ay, let 'em hang themselves, and then they are cold Meat for the Devil.

Capt. But, noble Champion, I hope we may have leave to roast the Rump to night.

Lov. With all our Hearts, here's Mony to make Fires—

Free. And here's for Drink to't, Boys.

All. Hey— Viva le Roy, viva les Heroicks! [Go out hollowing.

Enter Ananias peeping, Felt–maker, and Joyner.

Ana. So, the Rabble's gone: ah, Brethren! what will this wicked World come to?

Felt. Alack, alack, to no Goodness, you may be sure: pray what's the News?

[Fleet. peeping out of a Garret–Window.

Fleet. Anania, Anania!

Ana. Who calleth Ananias? lo, here am I.

Fleet. Behold, it is I, look up. How goeth tidings?

Ana. Full ill, I fear; 'tis a bad Omen to see your Lordship so nigh Heaven; when the Saints are Garretified.

Fleet. I am fortifying my self against the Evil–Day.

Ana. Which is come upon us like a Thief in the night; like a Torrent from the Mountain of Waters, or a Whirlwind from the Wilderness.

Fleet. Why, what has the Scotch General done?

Ana. Ah! he playeth the Devil with the Saints in the City, because they put the Covenant–Oath unto him; he pulls up their Gates, their Posts and Chains, and enters.

Felt. And wou'd the wicked City let him have his beastly Will of her?

Ana. Nay, but she was ravish'd— deflower'd.

Joy. How, ravish'd! oh monstrous! was ever such a Rape committed upon an innocent City? lay her Legs open to the wide World, for every Knave to view her Nakedness?

Felt. Ah, ah! what Days, what Times, and what Seasons are here? [Exeunt.

Enter Capt. Corp. and Prent. with Faggots, hollowing.

Corp. What say you now, Lads, is not my Prophecy truer than Lilly's? I told you the Rump would fall to our handling and drinking for: the King's proclaim'd, Rogues.

Capt. Ay, ay, Lilly, a Plague on him, he prophesied Lambert should be uppermost.

Corp. Yes, he meant perhaps on Westminster Pinacle: where's Lilly now, with all his Prophecies against the Royal Family?

Capt. In one of his Twelve Houses.

1 Pren. We'll fire him out to Night, Boy; come, all hands to work for the Fire. [Ex. all hollowing.

Fleet. Ah, dismal, heavy day, a day of Grief and Woe, Which hast bereft me of my hopes for ay, Ah, Lard, ah what shall I do? [Exit.

SCENE IV. A Chamber in Lambert's House.

Enter Lov. leading L. Lam. in disguise, Page and

Gilliflower disguised, Lov. dressing her.

Lov. My Charmer, why these Tears, If for the fall of all thy painted Glories, Thou art, in the esteem of all good Men, Above what thou wert then? The glorious Sun is rising in our Hemisphere, And I, amongst the crowd of Loyal Sufferers, Shall share in its kindly Rays.

L. Lam. Best of thy Sex— What have I left to gratify thy Goodness?

Lov. You have already by your noble Bounty, Made me a Fortune, had I nothing else; All which I render back, with all that Wealth Heaven and my Parents left me: Which, tho unjustly now detain'd from me, Will once again be mine, and then be yours.

Enter Free.

Free. Come, haste, the Rabble gather round the House, And swear they'll have this Sorceress.

Lov. Let me loose among 'em, their rude officious Honesty must be punish'd.

L. Lam. Oh, let me out, do not expose thy Person to their mad Rage, rather resign the Victim. [Holds him.

Lov. Resign thee! by Heaven, I think I shou'd turn Rebel first.

Enter La. Des. disguised, and Tom with Jewels in a Box.

L. Des. With much ado, according to thy direction, dear Freeman, I have pass'd the Pikes, my House being surrounded; and my Husband demanded, fell down dead with fear.

Free. How, thy Husband dead!

L. Des. Dead as old Oliver, and much ado I got off with these Jewels, the Rabble swore I was one of the Party; and had not the honest Corporal convinc'd em, I had been pull'd to pieces.—— Come, haste away, Madam, we shall be roasted with the Rump else.

L. Lam. Adieu, dear Mansion! whose rich gilded Roofs so oft put me in mind of Majesty—— And thou, my Bed of State, where my soft Slumbers have presented me with Diadems and Scepters—— when waking I have stretch'd my greedy Arms to grasp the vanish'd Phantom! ah, adieu! and all my hopes of Royalty adieu.——

Free. And dare you put your self into my Protection? Well, if you do, I doubt you'll never be your own Woman again.

L. Des. No matter, I'm better lost than found on such occasions. [Exeunt.

SCENE V. A Street; a great Bonfire, with Spits, and Rumps roasting, and the Mobile about the Fire, with Pots, Bottles, Fiddles.

1 Pren. Here, Jack, a Health to the King.

2 Pren. Let it pass, Lad, and next to the noble General.

1 Pren. Ralph, baste the Rump well, or ne'er hope to see a King agen.

3 Pren. The Rump will baste it self, it has been well cram'd.

Enter Freeman, L. Des. Loveless, and L. Lam. Gill. Tom,

Pages, etc.

Cap. Hah, Noble Champion, faith, Sir, you must honour us so far as to drink the King's Health, and the noble General's, before you go.

Enter Wariston, drest like a Pedlar, with a Box about his Neck full of Ballads and Things.

War. Will ya buy a guedly Ballat or a Scotch Spur, Sirs? a guedly Ballat, or a Scotch Spur.—— 'Sbread, I's scapt hitherte weele enough, I's say'd my Crag fro stretching twa Inches longer than 'twas borne: will ya buy a Jack–line to roast the Rump, a new Jack Lambert Line?— or a blithe Ditty of the Noble Scotch General?— come buy my Ditties.

Cap. How, a Ditty o'th' General? let's see't, Sirrah.

War. 'Sbread, Sirs, and here's the guedly Ballat of the General's coming out of Scotland.

Cap. Here, who sings it? we'll all bear the bob.

[Wariston sings the Ballad, all bearing the Bob.

Enter Ananias crying Almanacks.

Ana. New Almanacks, new Almanacks.

Cap. Hah, who have we here? Ananias, Holder–forth of Clement's Parish?

All. Ha, a Traytor, a Traytor.

Lov. If I am not mistaken, this blithe Ballad–singer too was Chair–man to the Committee of Safety.

Cap. Is your Lordship turned Pedlar at last?

War. What mon I do noo? Lerd, ne mere Lerd than yar sel, Sir; wons I show 'em a fair pair of Heels. [Goes to run away, they get him on a Colt–staff, with Ananias on another, Fidlers playing Fortune my Foe, round the Fire.

Cap. Play Fortune my Foe, Sirrah.

Enter Hewson, drest like a Country Fellow.

Cor. Who are you, Sirrah? you have the mark o' th' Beast.

Hews. Who aye, Sir? Aye am a Doncer, that come a merry–making among ya—

Cap. Come, Sirrah, your Feats of Activity quickly then. [He dances; which ended, they get him on a Colt–staff, and cry a Cobler, a Cobler.

All. A Cobler, a Cobler.

Cap. To Prison with the Traytors, and then we have made a good Night's work on't. Then let's all home, and to the Powers Divine Pray for the King, and all the Sacred Line. [Exeunt.

EPILOGUE

Spoken by Lady Desbro

_The Vizor's off, and now I dare appear.

High for the Royal Cause in Cavalier;

Tho once as true a Whig as most of you,

Cou'd cant, and lye, preach, and dissemble too:

So far you drew me in, but faith I'll be

Reveng'd on you for thus debauching me:

Same of your pious Cheats I'll open lay,

That lead your Ignoramus Flock astray:

For since I cannot fight, I will not fail

To exercise my Talent, that's to rail.

Ye Race of Hypocrites, whose Cloak of Zeal

Covers the Knave that cants for Commonweal,

All Laws, the Church and State to Ruin brings,

And impudently sets a Rule on Kings;

Ruin, destroy, all's good that you decree

By your Infallible Presbytery,

Prosperous at first, in Ills you grow so vain,

You thought to play the Old Game o'er again:

And thus the Cheat was put upon the Nation,

First with Long Parliaments, next Reformation,

And now you hop'd to make a new Invasion:

And when you can't prevail by open Force,

To cunning tickling Tricks you have recourse,

And raise Sedition forth without Remorse.

Confound these cursed Tories, then they cry, [In a preaching tone.

Those Fools, those Pimps to Monarchy,

Those that exclude the Saints; yet open th' Door,

To introduce the Babylonian Whore.

By Sacred Oliver the Nation's mad;

Beloved, 'twas not so when he was Head:

But then, as I have said it oft before ye,

A Cavalier was but a Type of Tory.

The Curs durst then not bark, but all the Breed

Is much encreas'd since that good Man was dead:

Yet then they rail'd against the Good Old Cause,

Rail'd foolishly for Loyalty, and Laws;

But when the Saints had put them to a stand,

We left them Loyalty, and took their Land:

Yea, and the pious Work of Reformation

Rewarded was with Plunder, Sequestration.

Thus cant the Faithful; nay, they're so uncivil,

To pray us harmless Players to the Devil.

When this is all th' Exception they can make,

They damn us for our Glorious Master's sake.

But why 'gainst us do you unjustly arm?

Our small Religion sure can do no harm;

Or if it do, since that's the only thing,

We will reform when you are true to th' King.___

Printed in Great Britain
by Amazon